After the Deluge: Reimagining Leonardo's Legacy

An  School Monograph

Kim Tanzer, FAIA,
Dean and Edward E. Elson Professor

After the Deluge:
Reimagining Leonardo's Legacy

Four dialogues, two gatherings, and an exhibition demonstrate the value of applying practical imagination to the subject of water

Kim Tanzer, FAIA, Dean and Edward E. Elson Professor
in collaboration with Jody Kielbasa, Vice Provost for the Arts

University of Virginia School of Architecture, Charlottesville, 2014

Editor: Cynthia Smith
Design: Cally Bryant

Printed by the University of Virginia School of Architecture

University of Virginia School of Architecture
Campbell Hall PO Box 400122
Charlottesville, VA 22904

www.arch.virginia.edu

Supported by the Office of the Provost & the Vice Provost for the Arts

Funding provided by the Fiddlehead Fund and the U.Va. Arts Council

Cover Image:
Carlton Ward Jr/CarltonWard.com

table of contents

introduction

After the Deluge, a Demonstration of the Practical Imagination Applied to the Ecology of Water

In the 15th century, Leonardo da Vinci fused an artist's persuasive understanding of water with an engineer's reasoned response in his "Deluge" series of drawings and his proposal to contain the flooded Arno River. Since that time, science has moved to the center of human discourse while art and visualization have often been relegated to the realm of the merely illustrative, decorative, or entertaining. But persistent catch phrases, "a picture is worth a thousand words" and "the heart has reasons that reason knows not of" serve to remind us that art, too, is a persuasive form of logic.

This demonstration of the practical imagination—one exhibition, two gatherings, and four dialogues—is inspired by Leonardo's synthetic approach to problem solving. The subject of the demonstration, water and the varied ways it epitomizes the challenges of environmental sustainability, was chosen because water is ubiquitous on the blue planet, and research and creative work on the subject is widespread across the University of Virginia, and the greater Academy.

"After the Deluge" was held during the Spring 2013 semester. Hosted by the School of Architecture, it incorporated artists and scientists from across Grounds who were paired with nationally recognized artists or scientists. The intended audiences include the participants from across Grounds and their students. "After the Deluge" contributed to a year-long effort of the School to focus on the subject of water. For the larger effort, see "drink" at www.arch.virginia.edu/resources/all-school-research-focus-water

An Exhibition: AQUIFERious VIRGINIA

February-May 2013 in the Dean's Gallery, with gallery talk March 29

Margaret Ross Tolbert, painter, with contributions from Eric Hutcheson, karst cartographer.

See www.aquiferious.com/about.html

Two Gatherings:

January 23, 12:30-2:00

April 23, 12:30-2:00

At the beginning and end of the project a gathering for on-Grounds participants was held at Open Grounds, a community meeting space on the University of Virginia grounds. Approximately 30 faculty members from across the University, including but not limited to those invited to participate in the dialogues, were invited, along with key academic leaders.

Four Dialogues:

The titles of the second, third, and fourth dialogues were borrowed from Seth McDowell's proposal to organize publication of *The Water Index*, the School of Architecture's 2012-13 DRINK project. His discussion of this means of organizing the School's efforts follows.

Reimagining Leonardo's Legacy
January 29-30, 2013

The Rising
February 19-20, 2013

The Contaminated
March 17-21, 2013

The Disappearing
March 28-29, 2013

"The Rising, the Contaminated, the Disappearing"

Seth McDowell, Assistant Professor of Architecture, University of Virginia

"Few challenges facing America and the world are more urgent than combating climate change. The science is beyond dispute and the facts are clear. Sea levels are rising. Coastlines are shrinking. We've seen record drought, spreading famine, and storms that are growing stronger with each passing hurricane season. Delay is no longer an option. Denial is no longer an acceptable response. The stakes are too high, the consequences, too serious. "

-Barack Obama
November 18, 2008
Bi-partisan Governors Global Climate Summit in Los Angeles, California

Hieronymus Bosch's *Deliverance from the Deluge*, painted on the inside of an altarpiece, reveals an image of a post-apocalyptic landscape. The water has subsided and rotting corpses of drowned sinners litter the land. This Old Testament depiction deploys water as a device for ethical cleansing, but if the moral connotations are ignored, the Deluge in Genesis 8 is essentially a story of technological adaptation to imposing natural phenomena. The Ark was a constructed response for survival. It has become the archetypal reply to ecological disaster: construct a mechanism for deliverance.

In the wake of an escalating global crisis with water we are searching for new mechanisms for deliverance. The seas are rising, the deserts are expanding, and the cities are growing at alarming rates. Anxiety is only elevated by the onslaught of extreme weather in the form of super-storms, hurricanes, tsunamis, landslides, floods, and droughts whose frequencies and intensities continue to increase. Couple this ever-present exposure to disaster with scientific data that suggests a future characterized by climate change and population growth and we have the ingredients for full-fledged paranoia. Water, our indispensable resource, is a dangerous and powerful element when it reaches towards states of imbalance.

The rising, the contaminated and the disappearing are three extremes for water. We can visually read the effects of these hydrological extremes both in the water and the context. It was suggested to use these three extremes as a thematic organization strategy for the *After the Deluge Symposium* at the University of Virginia's School of Architecture in the Spring of 2013 because while they each offer a water specific lens, they also provide an open framework for interpretation. The rising, refers to conditions of flooding or excess water and can be examined through methods for controlling rivers, arctic ice melt, and the future of cities and coasts relative to sea level rise. The contaminated, refers to the struggle to maintain healthy water quality. This topic leads to discussions in aquatic life, petrochemicals, waste treatment and urban run-off. Finally, there is the disappearing, which refers to water's ability to vanish. This topic could be interpreted as either water's disappearance by means of evaporation or water's capacity to erode the land, leading to discussions on drought, wetlands, erosion and underground aquifers.

After the Deluge offered a stimulating format for isolating these three stressed conditions and proved that it is very difficult to talk about the topics as mutually exclusive events. Flooding, contamination and disappearance can all be seen within one hydrological tragedy. In fact, these three actions are the ingredients of the epic Deluge of Genesis.

The Hell and the Flood (triptych from *Deliverance from the Deluge*), Hieronymus Bosch (circa 1450–1516).
Oil, 27.2 × 15.4", Rotterdam, Museum Boijmans Van Beuningen.

one

The Demonstration: Fluidity

"Infinite Slowness and Infinite Velocity in Leonardo's Water Studies"

Leslie Geddes, Ph.D. Candidate in Art History, Princeton University

"It is in the power of movement to extend to infinite slowness and likewise to infinite velocity."

Leonardo da Vinci, from the Codex Arundel 176 verso

Geddes used this provocative insight to compare the many ways Leonardo da Vinci interrogated water, saying she was concerned not with compartmentalization of Leonardo's fascinations with water, but rather with what she described as "shared causes." Her presentation revealed the many facets of his studies, and skillfully made linkages across scales, between media and study methods, and through time. Geddes spoke of da Vinci's water studies in three ways: engineering drawings intended to control the flow of water; geological studies of rock formations, indicating evidence of water's "infinite slowness"; and analytic studies of water's flow, suggesting its "infinite velocity." She discussed each in turn. She described his work on the cataclysmic effects of water—the later-named "Deluge" drawings—as itself a deluge, a torrent of information. In all, da Vinci produced 6000 pages of notes on this theme, still in existence.

The audience was introduced to da Vinci's work through a 1473 landscape drawing of the Arno Valley, the first such landscape drawing known in the tradition of western representation. Geddes highlighted the important role of water in this landscape, in the form of a turbulent waterfall in the foreground and a river coursing through the valley in the background. She said the drawing demonstrated water to

Landscape, 1473, Gabinetto Disegni e Stampe degli Uffizi.

be a "physical force of enormous potential and occasionally terrible consequences."

She then began a methodical discourse on da Vinci's engineering proposals devoted to water management. In this realm his design efforts ranged in scale from regional earth shaping projects such as a canal to bypass the city of Pisa, to machines to pump water, to bridges to span rivers. While the civil projects occur in the form of maps demonstrating large scale interventions, embedded in large if simplified contexts, Geddes characterized the machines as excerpted from physical context. She argued that they did not depict water at all, though the manipulation of water was clearly their absent

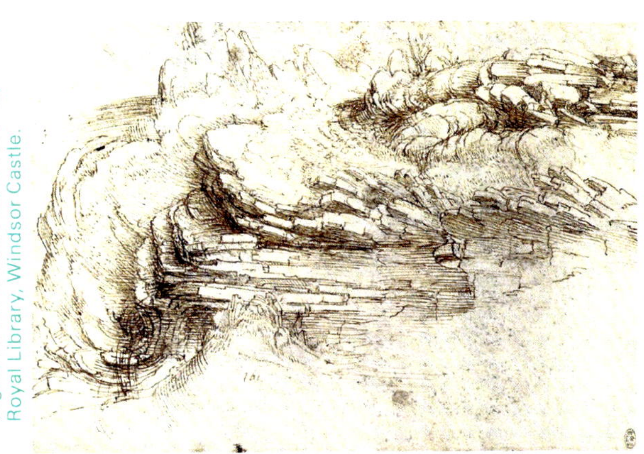

(left) Map of the Arno River, 1502-04, Royal Library, Windsor Castle. (right) Rock formations, c. 1510-13, Royal Library, Windsor Castle.

subject. Da Vinci's map of the Arno, she argued, demonstrated water both as a natural force and a force to be tamed.

She next turned her attention to the other kinds of drawings of water found in da Vinci's notebooks, starting with his studies of rock formations in relation to hydrological processes. Demonstrating his fascination, she said that da Vinci "describes water cutting through mountain passes as it wears away river beds and transports rocks and soil to alluvial planes in a constant process of landscape transformation." She observed that his studies of natural landscapes focused on sites of persistent change through the power of water, and that they also encompassed the broader visual problems of the representation of the passage of time. In studying rock formations, Geddes believed da Vinci analyzed not just external appearances but, indirectly, the underlying structures and dynamic processes of water.

On several occasions, Geddes points to the important role of da Vinci's artistic media, including the viscosity of ink mimicking the flow of a river, or the minerals in paint, made of the same substance as the subject being painted. The deep integrity of subject matter and study medium, translated through da Vinci's eye and hand, was a particularly subtle and powerful element in Geddes argument.

Geddes then turned to a discussion of the flow of water in da Vinci's work. Because the flow of water is fleeting (of "infinite velocity," in da Vinci's words Geddes described these analytic drawings as compelling graphic abstractions, often generated through observational studies, and often containing verbal or mathematical notations along with images.

She focused on several types of experiments he did to make visual, for himself and for his notes, the flow of water. One type of experiment began with a board inserted into a flowing current, leading to a particular, manipulable turbulence. Using the board as an obstacle to change water's shape, da Vinci also manipulated time. Here, she argued, he sought to record the sequence of water's movement. The waves, Geddes asserted, posed for da Vinci a geometric problem. She made mention of a diagram, studying the roll of turbulent waters over each other with the use of sequential letters to explain the path of the wave through time. Obstacle studies such as this led da Vinci to compare turbulent water to braided hair.

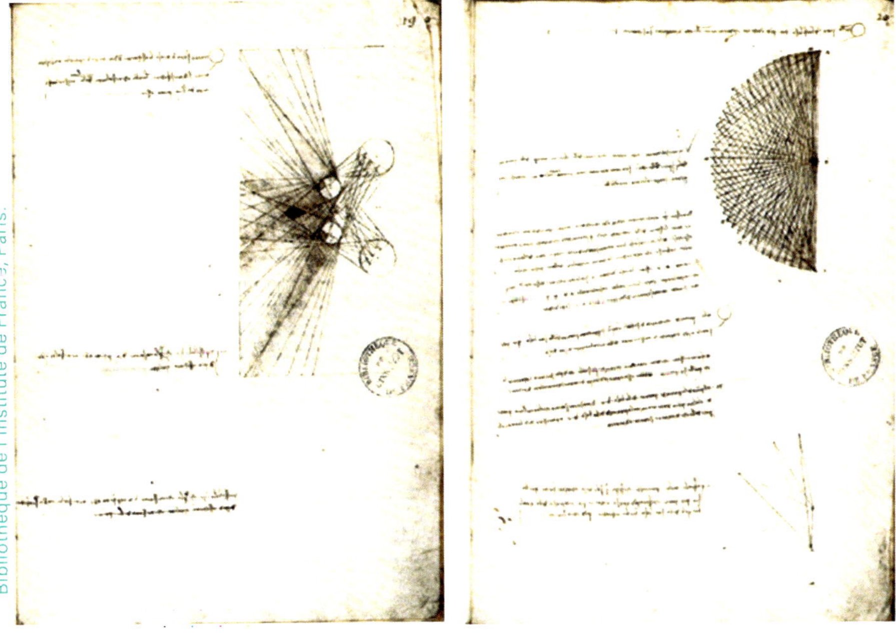

(left) Leonardo, Manuscript C, Folio 19r, Refraction of orbs, Bibliotheque de l'Institute de France, Paris.
(right) Leonardo, Manuscript, Refraction in the orbit of the sky, Bibliotheque de l'Institute de France, Paris.

Another type of study involved the use of millet seed, dropped into boiling water. Just as dust or smoke are used to give substance to otherwise invisible air, millet seed allowed da Vinci to see turbulence in action. Here, he could observe the roiling water through a glass sided vessel, studying water's action through a sectional view. As an aside, Geddes referred to da Vinci's designs for breathing devices and proto-scuba equipment, which would have allowed a person to descend in water to understand its vertical dimension from within—to see in water rather than simply to move through it.

Geddes ended her presentation with the "Deluge" drawings, done between 1515 and 1516, at the end of da Vinci's life. Depicting disaster, these chalk drawings present a tempest over a valley, the collapse of a mountainside, and violent swirls of water. She suggested that they fused an artist's imagining with a keen understanding of scientific processes. Whereas rock formations are the results of former catastrophic upheavals, the "Deluge" drawings point both backwards to the history of disaster and to future environmental calamities.

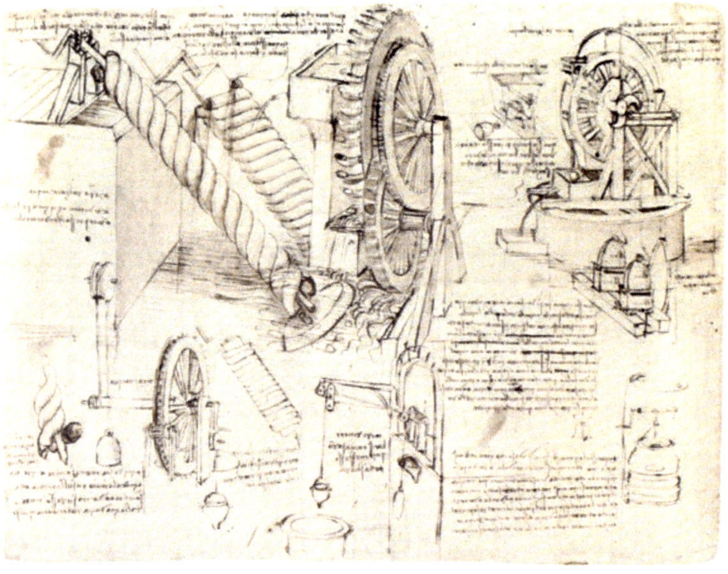

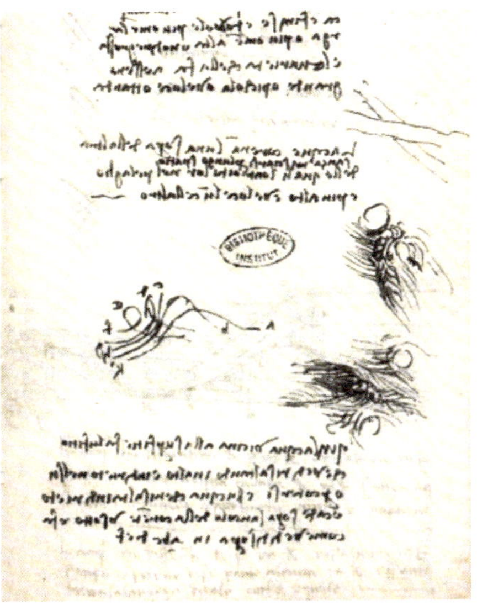

She concluded her presentation by bringing her audience back to da Vinci's 1483 painting "Virgin of the Rocks." Completing time's cycle, Geddes focused on the symbolic role of water, combining primordial rocks as evidence of destruction and in combination with the painting's other subject matter, as a source of renewal.

(left) Codex Atlanticus 26 verso, 1483, Biblioteca Ambrosiana.
(top right) Manuscript F 20 recto, c. 1508-13, Institut de France.
(bottom right) Deluge, c. 1515-16, Royal Library, Windsor Castle.

Francesca Fiorani, Associate Professor of Art History, University of Virginia

Leonardo da Vinci's fascination with atmospheric water—mist, clouds, rain—was the subject of Fiorani's talk. She began by articulating da Vinci's questions: Why is air sometimes more blue or less blue? What is the cause of mist? She noted his fascination with what we today call the physics of water—how water rises through the heat of the sun and then falls back to earth as rain. It rises with heat, cold air may cause it to freeze, and immobility "corrupts" it.

Her focus was on the state of water that "does not flow." She showed several drawings that demonstrate his fascination with swamps (water mixed with earth), with distant misted landscapes (water mixed with air), and with gigantic reflective surfaces made of water vapors and droplets. This, she explained, was da Vinci's artistic quest. He gave consistent attention to "floating water", mountains seen through fog, in drawings and rendered through color technique in paintings.

In the 1490s, as he painted the "Virgin of the Rocks," with its misted landscape, he also graphically represented theories of optics and of water. His rendition of a skyvault, a giant curved surface constructed of precise reflections, and his studies of spheres, occurred in the same manuscript with his first studies of flowing water.

Fiorani brought together da Vinci's quest, which she described as research on atmosphere, with his careful renderings of the properties of water, such as the "Deluge" drawings, to present a balanced presentation of his focused study with the subject of water.

(right) Leonardo da Vinci, Annunciation, 1472-75. (next page) Leonardo da Vinci, Annuciation 1473-75, detail, Uffizi Gallery, Florence, Italy.

Hossein Haj-Hariri
Chair and Professor of Mechanical and Aerospace Engineering, University of Virginia

Leonardo was one of the first engineers, argued Hossein Haj-Hariri, because he asked first "how" then "how can we improve things and make things that don't exist."

Haj-Hariri shared his own imaginings as he watched earlier presentations of the "Deluge" drawings. He said, "I actually go into the flow. I am actually a particle in that flow that he has drawn. I'm experiencing the stretch. I'm experiencing the turning. I'm intertwining with my neighboring particles and we're all moving. I actually have my hands held out this way, and depending on how the flow goes, maybe my hands come close together, maybe I'm rotating..."

Following this surprising personal observation, Haj-Hariri reflected that engineering is imagination "layered" onto scientific observation. He then discussed the importance of developing tools to do things differently.

Car design serves as an example of the interrelationship between tools and design. Starting in the 1930s he asserts that cars were aerodynamic, through the 1960s. In the 1980s, with the introduction of early CAD (computer aided design), cars became "boxy" and "ugly." Now, as CAD has become more powerful, cars can be beautiful again.

In conclusion, Haj-Hariri spoke of his work with 3-D printing, working with local school children. He said that tools are becoming more transparent and accessible to all, and that creativity is becoming democratized.

As a postscript, he added that while Leonardo did not use mathematical equations available today, they should not be viewed as separate from imagination. They are just shorthand for the text that Leonardo developed. The 18th century mathematician Leibniz invented the notations for calculus, which is still used today, allowing for the translation of Leonardo's text into its mathematical shorthand.

Nana Last
Associate Professor of Architecture, University of Virginia

Last began her presentation by describing the beginning of her interest in fluidity. She recounted her thoughts as they arose during an architecture review in which projects were discussed as "constructing, enacting, and ordering flows." She reflected on the well known observation by Justice Oliver Wendell Holmes, who said that the limit of free speech was yelling fire in a crowded theater. At this moment, she understood that the exiting flow of panicked patrons "transformed the speech-action dichotomy into a speech-action-space complex."

At the same time she began to question the liberal use of the term "flow" in architectural discourse. She asked, "What is it that flows? Is it the material or the inhabitants that are flowing? Is it that which directs and structures space or the space itself? Does architecture's materiality form flows, or form channels or markers of flows? And what relation, if any, do these ambiguities bear on the construct of fluidity itself?"

While giving examples of current architectural projects that are typically described as embodying flow or expressing fluidity, Last posited another premise, which she described as the "boson theory of flow." In contrasting SANAA's Rolex Learning Center in Lausanne, Switzerland, with the CERN Large Hadron Collider, she pointed to an architectural project built specifically to accommodate flows, suggesting an avenue for the explanation of fluidity aligned with current physics.

After a brief discussion of subatomic particle theory, and the important recent discovery of the Higgs boson particle, she explained the scientific concept of the boson, a "force carrying particle" as distinct from the fermion, a "matter carrying particle." She argued that "fluidity develops in architecture as a complex entity spanning material and nonmaterial systems and forces, including individual agency and social forms of agreement."

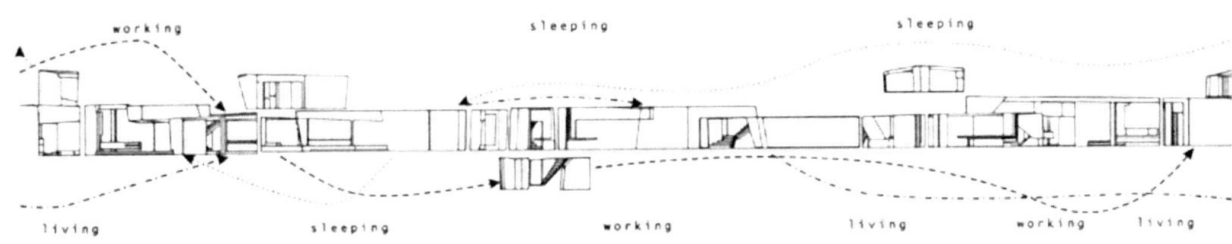

(previous page) Ben Van Berkel - Möbius House [UN Studio].
(left) Galaxy Soho, Zaha Hadid. Beijing, China.
(right) Standard Model of Elementary Particles.

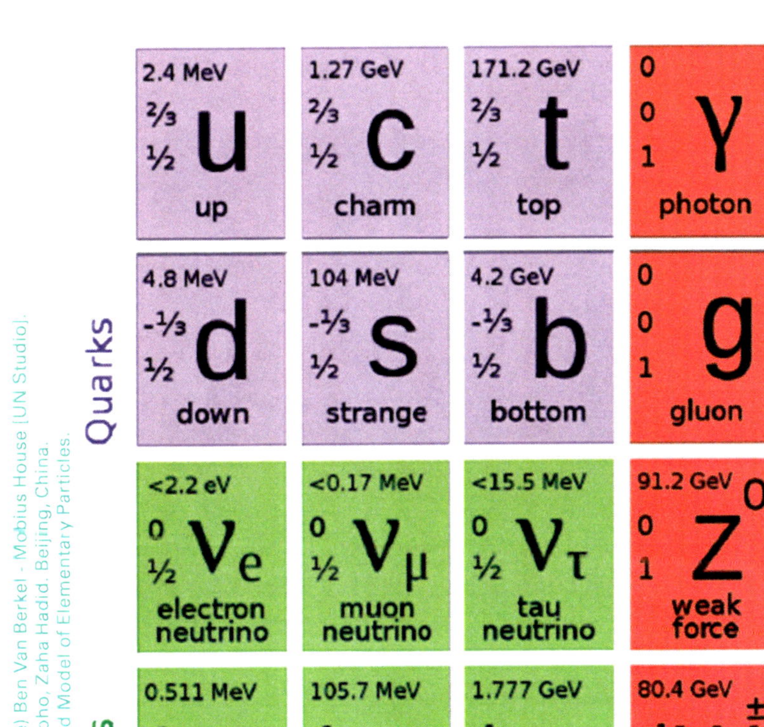

Matthew Reidenbach
Associate Professor of Environmental Sciences,
University of Virginia

Reidenbach argued that there are many scales of fluid motion, ranging from the entire ocean to the smallest of micro-organisms. Depending upon the size of the body in flow, relative to the velocity of the flow, things look very different. As a result, different bodies require different mechanisms to move in their environments.

He began his presentation with an image of the currents of the North Atlantic Ocean, followed by a reference to the Navier-Stokes equation that determines the movement of fluids. He then moved to an example of Panulirus argus, the spiny lobster, explaining how it detects odors (carried in an odor plume). He described a laboratory experiment using an odor plume, then showed a short film of a dye plume in an ocean current. He ended with an example of the microscopic Nudibranch larva which lives in Kane'ohe Bay, Hawaii. In this case, the larva adjusts its movement, dropping into a vertical position, when it senses chemical dispersion from a coral reef. He showed another film, demonstrating the way these tiny creatures navigate in a fluid environment.

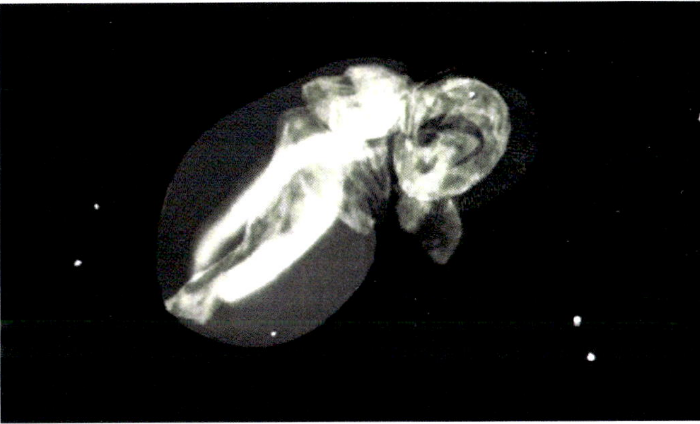

(top left) Kane'ohe Bay, Hawaii.
(top right and bottom) Nudibranch larva.

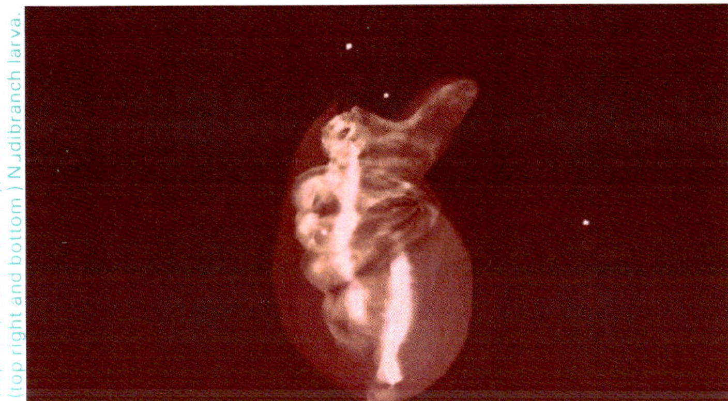

The Rising

"Creative Exploration on the Material Transformation of Water"

Matthew Burtner, Associate Professor of Composition and Computer Technologies, University of Virginia

Burtner's keynote began with an acoustic introduction: as audience members flowed into the room, a portion of the eco-acoustical composition "Ice Prints" played. On the screen, a 2008 image of Burtner paddling a kayak adjacent to Alaska's Mendenhall Glacier greeted the audience. Burtner began his presentation by explaining that as the photograph was being taken he was paddling furiously to overcome the current created by the rapidly melting glacier. This troubling anecdote set the tone for Burtner's presentation.

The first three components of his presentation were summaries of recent evidence of melting glaciers and resultant sea level rise. He began with a video clip of Al Gore presenting his now-famous powerpoint presentation. The portion shown began with graphic evidence of glaciers melting in Greenland, then followed with a series of highly populated coastlines, showing how they would be inundated using the sea level rise data presented by Gore. San Francisco, Beijing, Shanghai,

Calcutta, Manhattan, along with the Netherlands and the Florida peninsula were used to demonstrate the catastrophic human impacts of sea level rise. Gore suggested that up to 100 million people might be displaced, reminding his audience of the horrific impact of even 100 thousand climate refugees.

Next Burtner discussed the work of photographer James Balog, whose 2012 documentary "Chasing Ice" describes glacial melt and sea level rise with less alarming data but an equal sense of urgency. Balog presents three years' of glacial retreat through his photographs. Burtner refers to a TED Talk (Technology, Entertainment, Design) where Balog furthers this assessment.

Burtner made reference to a powerful trend written about by University of Colorado scientists and captured over a seven year period by NASA's Gravity Recovery and Climate Experiment (GRACE) project, which captured data from 200,000 glaciers worldwide between 2007-10. He says that during this time sea level

rose by one half inch, and the lost ice equaled 4.3 trillion tons of water. Burtner said that he saw European cruise ships in Barrow, Alaska because, now, for the first time, the Northwest Passage had become virtually ice free. He further described the inundation of some low lying islands in the central Pacific Ocean, and that Samoans had been forced to relocate to higher ground. Burtner cited another 2010 study suggesting that a two degree rise in temperature by 2300 would lead to a sea level rise of between 1.5 and 4 meters. While less dramatic than Al Gore's data indicated, this would nonetheless cause substantial human disaster.

Following this scientific preamble, Burtner shifted to a discussion of his own work as a composer. He began by describing his fascination with the transformative quality of water as an artistic medium, from solid ice to liquid water to gas. He expressed interest, too, in the human role in this drama, saying, "We are not only the cause and the effect of this process of rising, but we are part of it."

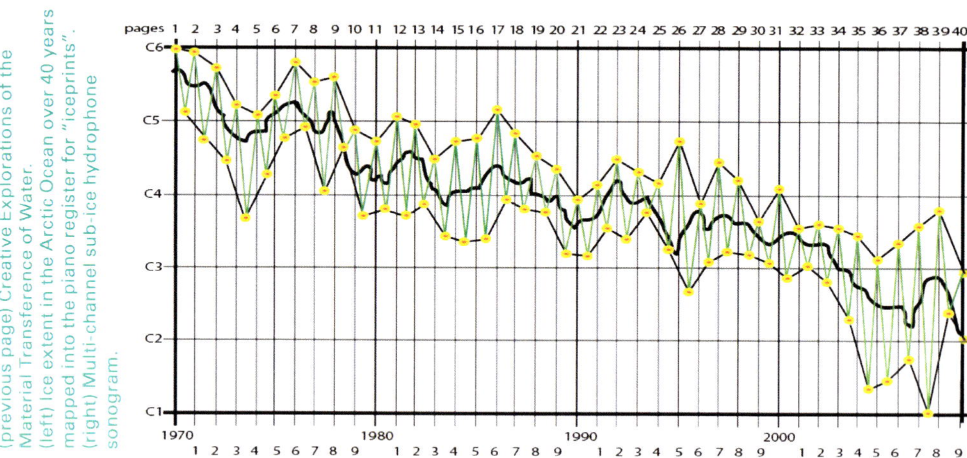

(previous page) Creative Explorations of the Material Transference of Water.
(left) Ice extent in the Arctic Ocean over 40 years mapped into the piano register for "iceprints".
(right) Multi-channel sub-ice hydrophone sonogram.

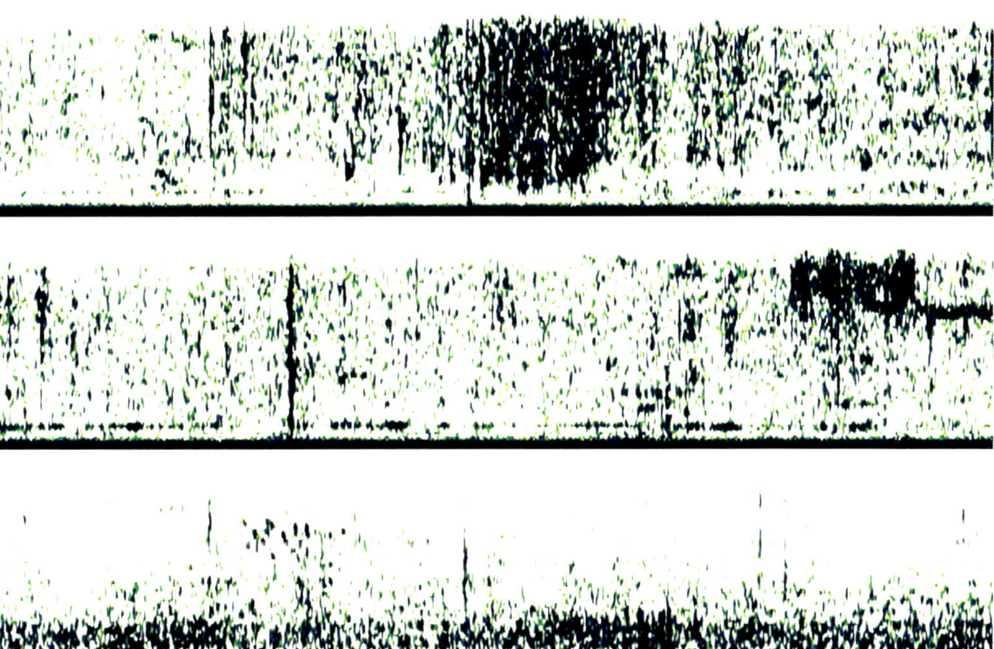

He showed a graph of the extent of ice, thawing and refreezing in an annual cycle over a period representing forty years. He noted that the trend, showing total remaining ice, is downward over this time. He explained that he overlaid this graph on a piano register and used it as the foundation of a musical composition, called "Ice Prints," created for piano and sub-ice acoustics. He showed his recording process, with recording devices mounted on the bow of his kayak and underwater, and played a further recording with three hydrophones collecting sound underwater at intervals of one mile apart. In his translational notation system, the sound of cracking ice signified a particular piano tone. The piece was performed with surround sound—one piano and two speakers, so the audience experience could be spatialized. Further electro-acoustical manipulations were introduced in a systematic way.

He next spoke of his opera, Auksalaq, and showed a portion of a video of this piece, which incorporated piano, flute, voice, xylophone, and bowls of ice with sampled sound. He ended with a quote by the opera's narrator: "The networks of oceans, lakes, streams, interlock the planet. All that water, freezing and thawing, vaporizing and condensing over us, under us, around us, and in us. Our bodies are made mostly of water. We humans are also a substantial body of water—part of that network. Our tide of billions pulls one way, and earth shifts."

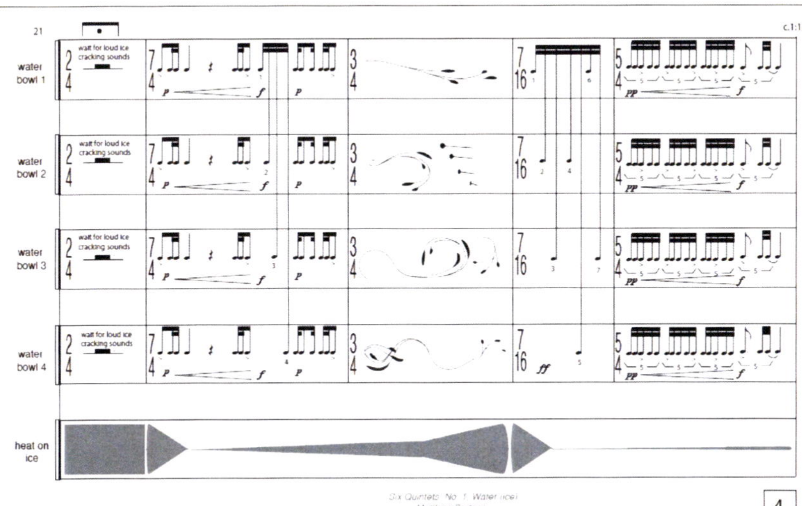

(top) Six Ambient Extensions: No. 1, Water (ice).
(bottom) In Auksalaq, Ice Prints is combined with similar ecoacoustic systems for clouds and wind, into a multilayered ecosystem of sound. Image by Scott Deal.

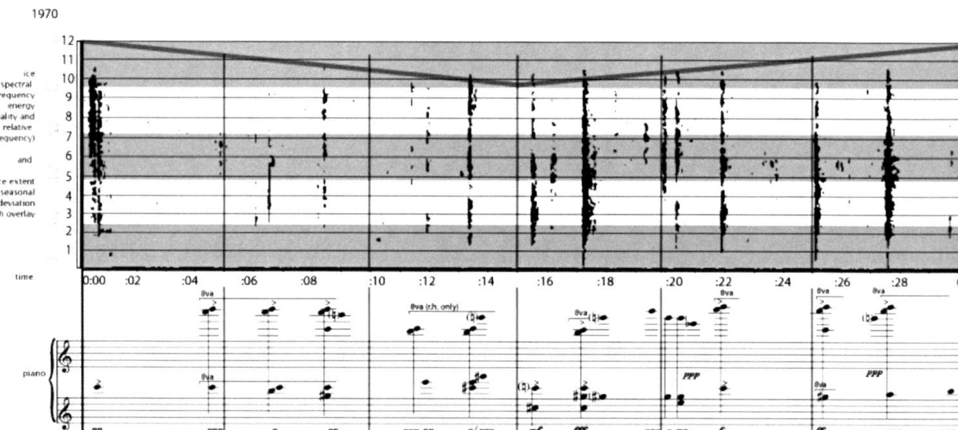
1970
ice spectral frequency energy (quality and relative frequency)
and
ice extent seasonal deviation graph overlay
time
0:00 :02 :04 :06 :08 :10 :12 :14 :16 :18 :20 :22 :24 :26 :28
8va
8va (r.h. only)
piano
ped
sustain pedal throughout
ice spectral amplitude energy (dynamics)

(left) "Ice Prints" - The piano is a transcription of one hydrophone recording.
(right) Six Ambient Extensions: No. 1. Water (ice).

Iñaki Alday
Chair and Quesada Professor of Architecture, University of Virginia

Alday's presentation posited that water is a powerful "material" and suggests, through examples of flooding and his architectural firm's (Alday/Jover) project, Zaragoza Water Park, that this powerful material is amenable to manipulation, but not control. He began with two examples of 17th century cities, Rome and London, each of which came to understand its respective river, the Tiber and the Thames, as each city's "backyard" where filth, moral decay, and all things undesirable were located. He pointed to the design of the Isola Tibera as a "boat island" floating safely above the water, well anchored to solid banks.

He provided other historic examples of near-mythic flooding along the Nile and the Mississippi. The first historic, though often overlooked example, is the Nile River flooding and its beneficial role in fertilizing the delta for agricultural use. A "Nile-o-Meter" measures the height of the flooded river. The second, more recent example, is the Mississippi River. He showed the mapping of the Army Corps of Engineers containment strategies following the 1927 floods, and the built evidence of their work in the form of levees, some now or then breached.

He characterized the strategies used to control the Mississippi as "hard engineering solutions" intended to control the river's dynamics.

Levee failure, Greenville, Mississippi.

Taking a metaphoric interlude, he reflected on a personal source of inspiration, bullfighting. He suggested that as water is a material for his architectural firm, the torero, Luis Francisco Espla, believes the bull is his "material of creation." He quoted Espla, saying in part, "To understand how to create with the bull, we should approach the concept of material...probably there is no other artistic discipline which relies on the subtraction of the will of the material or is based on the will of the material."

As a response to these circumstances—the dynamic, material willfulness of water, Alday presented the 2008 Water Park in Zaragoza, intended to absorb and celebrate occasional fierce flooding. This project, with shallow decorative/pragmatic ponds of slightly varying depth, changes its form with varying degrees of water surges.

(left) The Water Park, Zaragoza 2008 Flood June 2008, 1.555 m^3/sg.
One week before EXPO opening ceremony.
(right) Bullfighting: bull as "material".

Leena Cho and Matthew Jull
Visiting Assistant Professor of Landscape Architecture and Assistant Professor of Architecture, University of Virginia

In their presentation, Cho and Jull discussed their design research, focused in the arctic region. They have sought to reverse the current question regarding global warming and sea level rise, asking instead, what opportunities will arise as climate change impacts the arctic? In particular, they are interested in economic opportunities that may become apparent to human populations that are often living in minimally viable circumstances. They have sought to "recenter" the world by placing the north pole and arctic region in the center of the map and, therefore, of their thinking. In this context, they propose that Greenland might be understood as a "mother cloud", that is, the center of a global data storage center, powered through the abundantly available hydropower that would be a by-product of sea level rise.

(top) Masterplan for the Greenland Mothercloud: Hydropower and data storage center network. Official Catalog for Danish Pavilion, The 12th Venice ArchitecturalBiennale.
(bottom) Proposed relationship between data centers, hydropower stations, and data transmissions on Greenland.

(left) Image by David Brosha.
(right) "Masterplan for the Greenland Mothercloud: Hydropower and data storage center network", Official Catalog for Danish Pavilion, The 12th Venice ArchitecturalBiennale.

Patricia Wiberg
Chair and Professor of Environmental Sciences, University of Virginia

The title of Wiberg's presentation was "Sea Level Rise: Reality, Uncertainty, and Controversy," and she summarized, in this neat format, the scientific community's shared understanding of both the known and more speculative elements of the theories of sea level rise. Beginning with "Reality," Wiberg reported that scientists agree that between 1950 and the year 2000 sea level has risen on average two millimeters per year, with one half coming from melting ice and one half from the expanded volume of warming water. She said that this rate has increased to three millimeters per year in the last 20 years. The "Uncertainty" in her report comes from the fact that many scientists believe two millimeters per year is a conservative estimate. She further suggested that the Antarctic ice sheet contains three to four times that much volume when ice is converted to water which then expands further as it warms. Finally she addressed the recently politicized use of the term "sea level rise" suggesting that some policy makers prefer the term "recurrent flooding" which occurs regularly in places like Norfolk ,Virginia during full moons and other natural cyclical events. She ended by reminding the audience that Hurricane

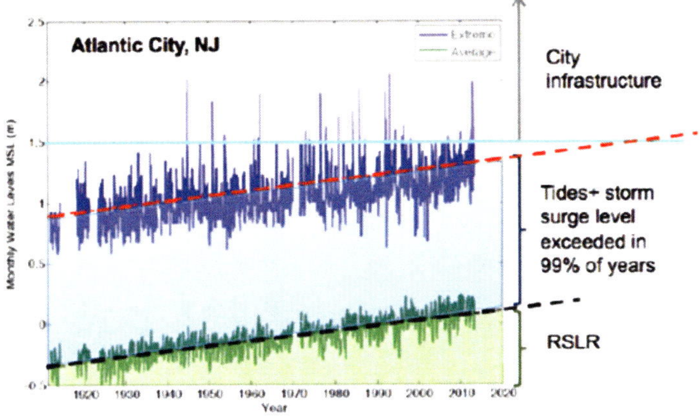

Sandy, which came ashore in the New Jersey-New York metropolitan area in October 2012, caused damage primarily due to a strong storm surge. She suggested that, whether called "sea level rise" or "recurrent flooding," storm events exacerbate already tenuous coastal shorelines, leading to catastrophic effects in densely settled areas. In this case, she argued that damage was caused by the combination of a strong storm surge, coastal flooding, and sea level rise.

(top) Sea level rise and increase in frequency of coastal flooding.
(bottom) Sea level rise: reality, uncertainty and controversy.

The Contaminated

"Praeter Naturam: Beyond Nature"

Brandon Ballengée
Artist, Biologist, and Visiting Scientist at McGill University

Ballengée operates equally as an artist and a scientist. In his presentation he discussed his scientific research on amphibians with missing or extra limbs, his efforts to train citizen scientists, and his own art practice. He brought focus to the 2010 Deepwater Horizon oil spill in the Gulf of Mexico and the resulting widespread contamination.

At the outset Ballengée asked rhetorically, "What is the contaminated?". He asserted that all people born after the industrial revolution, as well as animals, are contaminated. He followed this with a second question, "What is preternatural—beyond nature?". Here he began to unfold his own story, and his transdisciplinary efforts to link art and science.

At McGill University, he performs fieldwork and laboratory work, looking at amphibians as bioindicator species: groups of organisms that explain more broadly what is happening in local ecosystems. A life-long lover of amphibians, he became aware of the alarming trend in the late 1980s in which populations of frogs, toads and salamanders were said to have disappeared, a phenomenon which became known as the "amphibian apocalypse." He discussed two particularly disturbing trends, the increase of "extra limbs" and "missing limbs" among some populations.

Following an initial report of young frogs with limb malformations found by schoolchildren in Minnesota lakes, their biology teacher contacted the Environmental Protection Agency. The report was investigated further through the United States Geological Survey (USGS). Quickly it was realized that such reports go back centuries, while at the same time, media sources began arguing that pollution was the cause of this disturbing phenomenon. Scientists were soon forced into the media spotlight, with the public expectation that chemical pollution would be identified as the source of the deformities. Instead, a parasite called a trematode was identified. Ballengée explained that the parasite grows into tadpoles' limb buds where it absorbs into and damages tissues. Tadpoles respond, trying to regenerate the missing limb bud, leading to extra limbs. Ballengée explained that this is a mechanical phenomenon, not directly related to pollution. He tracked the life cycle of the parasite, wherein predators, such as herons, eat frogs immobilized by these severe deformities, and the parasites are ingested, then hatched to begin another food cycle, with snails as intermediate hosts. Ballengée carefully explained that parasites are "natural" but that parasites are known to increase in ponds with agricultural runoff. While chemicals do not directly lead to frog deformities, they do increase the incidence of such deformities indirectly.

He then explained the second type of deformity, missing limbs. This example, too, focuses on farm ponds. In this case, he determined that dragonfly nymphs selectively ate hind limbs, carefully selecting then chewing off and eating the legs. Again, Ballengée noted that predators such as dragonfly nymphs are "natural," but that the incidence of predation and the missing limb phenomenon was higher in farm ponds. He asserted that, where water is contaminated not all species thrive, but some species of dragonfly nymphs appear to. Because they are pollution tolerant, frogs with missing limbs, too, are more likely found in polluted farm ponds.

Through these two examples, Ballengée debunked two misperceptions. First, he clarified that chemical pollution does not

(left) Types of anuran hind limb deformities: "extra" limbs - increased occurrence in western United States. "missing" limbs- vast majority occur throughout North America and internationally.
(right) DFA 83: Karkinos. 2001/07. Unique iris print. In scientific collaboration with Stanley K. Sessions. Titles in collaboration with the poet KuyDelair. Courtesy the artist and Ronald Feldman Fine Arts, New York, NY.

necessarily lead directly to physical deformities, despite a public will to reach this conclusion. Second, by explaining scientists' processes in discovering the cause of these types of deformities, he helped non-scientists in the audience understand that scientists follow evidence wherever it leads, however unwelcome.

Ballengée then spoke briefly about his project to create citizen scientists through his temporary Public Bio-Art Laboratories. Either conducting field work with citizens, who expand the reach of data collection while learning scientific methods, or creating resource centers, such as research libraries or imaging labs for public use, Ballengée seeks to engage the public in the process of carefully understanding nature.

Through his own art, too, Ballengée seeks to bring awareness to the plight of creatures under siege in the post-industrial world. He described his art practice as carefully as his science, focusing first on a series of prints of frogs with missing or extra limbs. He said the process for each image might take two weeks to two months. He begins by clearing and staining a specimen, using digestive enzymes to make the specimen transparent. Then colored stains turn bones red and cartilage blue. This process, with 20 to 25 discrete steps, leads to a specimen that he carefully lays out to achieve aesthetic effect. Following a high-resolution scan, which can take 8 to 12 hours, the print is complete. Each print is three feet by four feet and is intended to be scaled to the size of a human toddler and to resemble the coloration and quality of a 19th century watercolor. He explained that if the image is too big, people become frightened, but if too small, people easily differentiated themselves from the subject. His goal is to help people empathize with each frog specimen, to think of them as individuals.

Concluding this segment of his talk, Ballengée showed images of the prints, and specimen/ sculptures in a gallery context. The installation, which he called Styx, referencing the mythical netherworld river between living and dead, showed a series of backlit individual frog specimens, which he hoped people would engage very directly.

(left) Gallery 400, Chicago, fall 2008. (right) Styx: Variation I. 2007. Yerba Buena Center for the Arts, San Francisco, California. Image by Phillip Ross.

Finally, Ballengée spoke of the BP oil spill in the Gulf of Mexico and its cleanup. He compared the publicity mounted by the BP oil company, and asserted that the cleanup had not been as successful as portrayed in media releases. He then described another installation "Collapse" at Ronald Feldman Gallery, which included a sculpture of greater than 500 jars representing the food pyramid in the Gulf and the species impacted by the spill, many of which are in decline. He spoke specifically of several species harmed by the spill, including: shrimp, born with mysterious lesions, missing eyes, and tissue asymmetries; baby dolphins washed ashore; and fish, indigenous to the Gulf of Mexico, for sale in markets in England following their migration with the Gulf Stream. The exhibition also included a comparison of BP advertisements with scientific knowledge of the spill, and a 400 page dossier downloadable from the Feldman Gallery website.

With this final art installation Ballengée moved from disturbing frog deformities caused only indirectly by chemical contamination to a global catastrophe directly attributable to human-caused pollution. Despite the elegance of his art, the story he told was bleak.

(left) DFA 186, Hades, 2012. Unique iris print. In scientific collaboration with Stanley K. Sessions. Courtesy the artist and Ronald Feldman Fine Arts, New York, NY.
(middle) Piedmont, Italy Eco-Action from 2010 Malamp IT studies. Image by Orietta Brombin, 2010.
(right) Host cycle diagram.

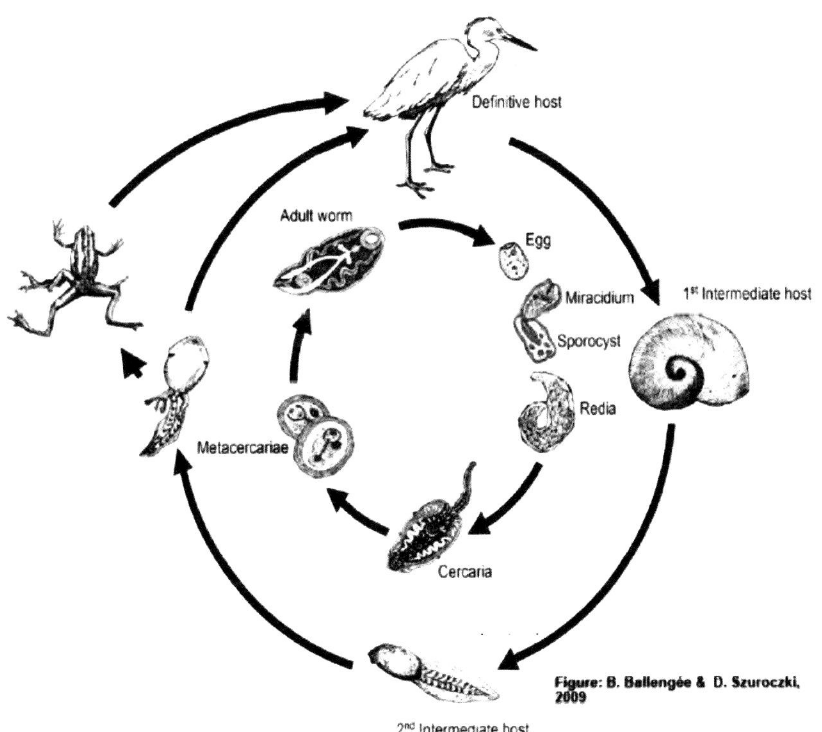

Figure: B. Ballengée & D. Szuroczki, 2009

Phoebe Crisman
Associate Professor of Architecture, University of Virginia

Crisman discussed a design project she has developed with several classes of School of Architecture students, focused on the Elizabeth River and the Chesapeake Bay. She began by describing the project's site in relation to her audience at the University of Virginia. Located two and a half hours from Charlottesville, this region has been impacted by generations of industrial activity and resulting contamination. Railways, oil storage, and other industrial uses—all an expected part of everyday contemporary life—have left these waterfront areas heavily polluted. Her projects, at Money Point and at the Paradise Creek Nature Park, are attempts to educate school children, in particular, about the value of healthy riparian ecosystems.

She spoke briefly about three projects, and identified the 40+ stakeholder groups with whom she and her students worked in designing and implementing these projects. The first project "16 silos, 16 shades of yellow" which she directed jointly with Architecture Professor Sanda Iliescu, announced the group's collective positive intentions with bold, brilliant yellow, free-flowing draped silos. Following this spectacular event, the second project, "The Learning Barge" was a unique design-build project, wherein

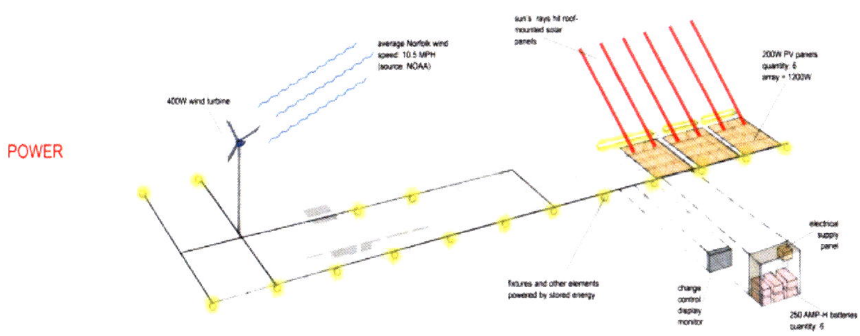
POWER
400W wind turbine
average Norfolk wind speed: 10.5 MPH (source: NOAA)
sun's rays hit roof-mounted solar panels
200W PV panels quantity: 6 array = 1200W
electrical supply panel
fixtures and other elements powered by stored energy
charge control display monitor
250 AMP-H batteries quantity: 6

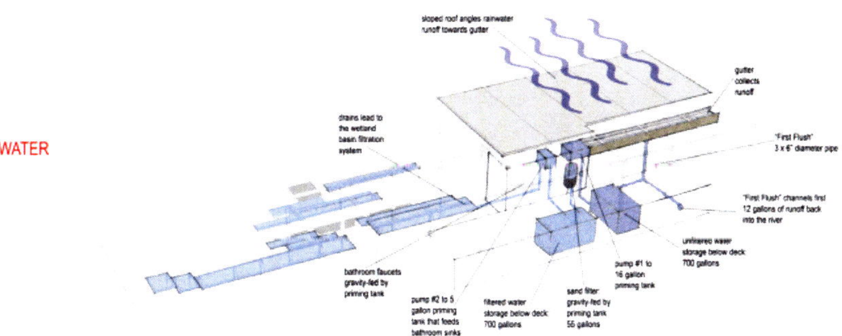
WATER
sloped roof angles rainwater runoff towards gutter
gutter collects runoff
drains lead to the wetland basin filtration system
"First Flush" 3 x 6" diameter pipe
"First Flush" channels first 12 gallons of runoff back into the river
unfiltered water storage below deck 700 gallons
pump #1 to 16 gallon priming tank
bathroom faucets gravity-fed by priming tank
pump #2 to 5 gallon priming tank that feeds bathroom sinks
filtered water storage below deck 700 gallons
sand filter gravity-fed by priming tank 55 gallons

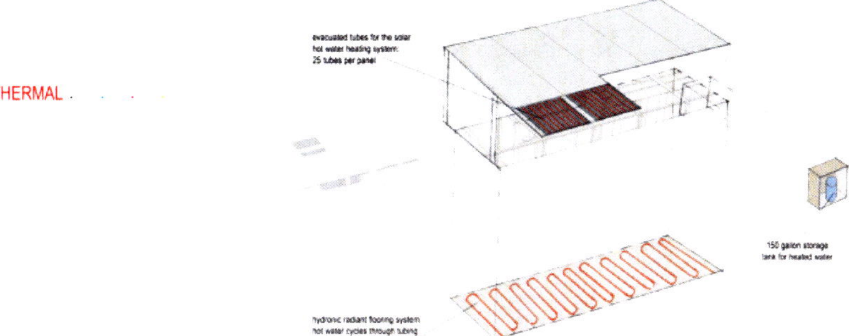
THERMAL
evacuated tubes for the solar hot water heating system: 25 tubes per panel
150 gallon storage tank for heated water
hydronic radiant flooring system hot water cycles through tubing embedded in classroom floor

Crisman and her students fabricated a barge, designed as a floating environmental classroom, moored on the Elizabeth River. As of the date of the presentation, more than 20,000 students had visited the Learning Barge to learn about strategies for cleansing water through collection and reuse strategies. The third project, "Paradise Creek Nature Park," had been commissioned by the Elizabeth River Project as a 30 acre wetland park, completely detached from urban infrastructures such as power and water. The students, working with Crisman, provided detailed designs which the consortium is working to implement.

(left) Money Point sustainable 10-year revitalization plan.
(right and next page) Learning Barge.

Rebecca Dillingham
Medical Doctor and Associate Professor, Medicine, Infectious Diseases and International Health, University of Virginia

Dillingham reported on her research, which focuses on a "natural" form of contamination, microbial contamination of water from human feces, which causes deadly diseases such as cholera, with initial symptoms including diarrhea and vomiting. She began with an historic reflection on the important work of British physician John Snow, considered the founder of modern epidemiology, who, working with citizen scientist Harry Whitehead, mapped the incidence of an 1831 cholera outbreak in London and linked it to a contaminated public well. She recognized the important outcome of this effort in the creation of London's sewer system.

She reflected on the futures of those infected who do not die from cholera, and described evidence of decreased size and cognitive capacity in those who survive. As a result, she argued that cholera has multigenerational effects, showing a self portrait of a girl without hands, indicating a loss of agency, or the capacity to control her own future.

(top left) Sudanese woman making ceramic water filter. Image by Frank Broadhurst, International Rescue Committee. (top right) Solar disinfection of drinking water.

Jim Smith
Professor of Civil and Environmental Engineering, University of Virginia

Following Dillingham's discussion of the importance of potable water for populations with minimal access to public infrastructure, Smith discussed his work on small scale water treatment systems in the developing world. Like Dillingham, he began by providing context, in his case global context rather than historic. He, too, argued that not only death, but stunted physical growth and cognitive impairment, are the tragic consequences of contaminated drinking water. He said one billion people lack access to improved water supplies, and 2.5 billion lack access to sanitation, making the problem of waterborne pathogens huge, and disproportionately impactful. He showed a strategically manipulated map of Guatemala to illustrate his point.

Following a directive of the World Health Organization, he has worked to create decentralized water treatment systems, also known as point-of-use treatment systems. He describes his work to create the "Madi Drop" technology, which has three components with escalating effectiveness. The first is a fired-clay filtration system that removes larger particulate matter. The second is the addition of Madi drops to contaminated water. Made with copper and silver ions these drops create an unfavorable chemical matrix which reduces the incidence of water born pathogens. The third, most effective strategy, combines the first two. In this case, water is filtered mechanically using a ceramic filter, further purified using Madi drops.

Approach: Filter and MadiDrop, porous ceramic, impregnated with silver/copper "nanopatches," meets design criteria.

The Disappearing

"AQUIFERious"

Margaret Ross Tolbert
Artist and Environmentalist, Gainesville, Florida

Painter Margaret Ross Tolbert spoke about her work—as a painter and activist—reflected in the recent history of North Central Florida's freshwater springs. She explained that there are more first magnitude freshwater springs in this part of Florida—more than 1,000 of varying sizes—than anywhere else in the world. She cited the early descriptions provided by naturalist William Bartram, who traveled to this area two centuries ago, and who described geysers of water shooting into the air from the underground pressure, the sound of which could be heard nearly a mile away. She noted that the springs Bartram encountered, sadly have diminished, and spent much of her talk describing and demonstrating their decline.

She exhibited photographs and video clips of springs taken by her and others; her paintings and performance pieces as Sirena; maps of Florida's springs; the Floridian aquifer, and springs recharge areas; and evidence of scientific studies of springs flow rates and nitrate saturation, among other scientific studies. In essence she gave several presentations simultaneously.

Beginning with a photograph and painting of Silver Glen Springs, located in the Silver Springs region near Ocala, one of Tolbert's narratives told the story of the decline of water quality and volume over her professional career. She

Ginnie Springs, Florida.

referenced Silver Glen Springs repeatedly, demonstrating its prior crystal clear water and abundant flow, and its more recent state, with profuse algae blooms as a result of nitrates entering the aquifer from dairy farms within the recharge area.

A second thread running through Tolbert's presentation was the balance of an artist's understanding of the springs and the growing understanding scientists have developed of this remarkable region. Her sensitivity to and experience with color and composition, with optical qualities like reflection and refraction, and her recognition of the role water plays in making small or invisible things visible within its matrix, are key to her practice as an artist. At the same time, she introduced the voices of several scientists, who describe the springs in terms of their chemical composition, flow rates, and spatial configurations. She referenced their work specifically through charts and maps.

(left) Peacock Springs, Image by Lesley Gamble. (right) Margaret Tolbert painting on site, Rainbow River, Image by Stefan Craciun.

Tolbert also showed her own work: a series of paintings of springs completed over several decades; installations in galleries and large institutional spaces such as airports and museums; and her staged photographs in which she performs as Sirena, an exceptional creature who rollerskates, bowls, and performs other special and everyday tasks under water. Tolbert paid particular attention to the experience of her audiences, helping them "sink into springs" while riding an escalator, float amidst springs in a room filled with large canvases, or experience refraction while viewing lenticular pieces (prismatic photomontages). She described her working process, from kayaking with a painting-ready "side car" to working in her outdoor studio, and sketching while swimming. In particular, her role as both observer and subject, working above, on, and in the springs, sets her work apart from other artists.

(left) Sirena Rollerskating, 2013, Image by Tom Morris.
(right) Juniper Sand Boils, 2007. Oil, 90x90".

She began and closed her talk with a call for action. She started with a description of her 2010 book, *AQUIFERious*, winner of the State of Florida Book Award, and quoted from it extensively throughout her presentation, explaining that the book was intended to use science to explain her artist's concern, and art to draw a new audience to science. She ended with a mention of a recent demonstration intended to prompt policy makers to take action, communicated via Facebook. She argued that, like the ancient, monumental Buddha statues of Bamiyan, destroyed by the Taliban in Afghanistan, Florida's springs are a treasure deserving of every possible effort to protect.

(left) Brimming Over, 2008, Oil.
(right) "Portals and Passages", The Arts Center, Northwest Florida College, Niceville, Florida, 1997. Image by Jack Gardner.

Paolo D'Odorico
Ernest H. Ern Professor of Environmental Sciences, University of Virginia

D'Odorico's presentation was organized around the parallel arguments of water disappearing over time, and in space. Beginning with the disappearance of water over time, he began by reminding the audience that evidence demonstrates that 6,000 years ago the Sahara Desert was wet and green. He said the Sahara's desertification coincides with the rise of human civilization.

He then gave other, more recent examples of formerly wet areas, particularly lakes, that have become significantly more arid during the course of the last century. He highlighted Badain Jaran Desert, Inner Mongolia, and China, noting former shorelines now evident as residual traces in the Gobi Desert; evidence of inland sand dunes in Southern Africa; and the paleolakes of Makgadikgadi Pan in Botswana. He cited other ephemeral lakes and pans, such as Tshane in Botswana, Lake Chad, the Aral Sea, Mar Chiquita in Cordoba, Argentina and Lake Orumieh in Iran, all of which are greatly reduced in volume even in recent decades.

Shifting to examples of "disappearance in space" he described the Okavango River in Angola, which no longer flows to the sea, disappearing instead into the sands of the Kalahari Desert.

He emphasized the role that river plays in providing habitat for plants and animals, supporting the region's biodiversity. He mentioned that planning efforts are underway to protect this important wetlands area, described as an inland delta.

Paleolakes: The Mokgadikgadi Pans, Botswana.

The Disappearance of Lake Chad in Africa

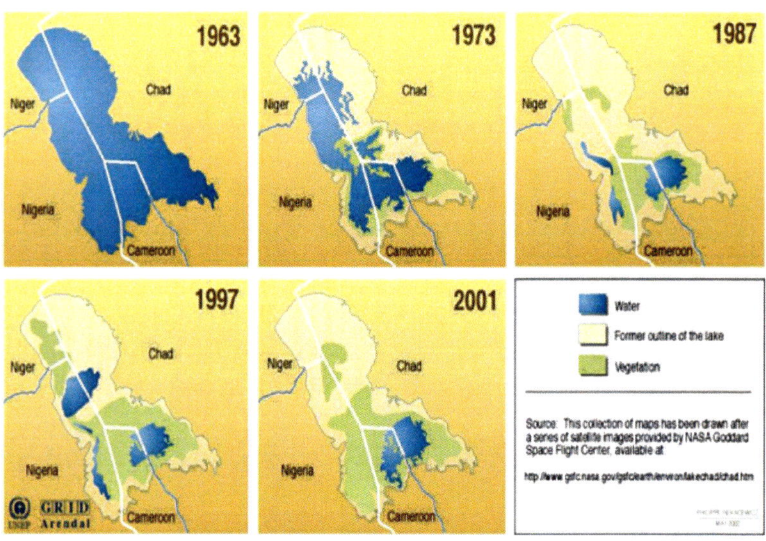

(left) The Disappearance of Lake Chad in Africa. Original image by Philippe Rekacewicz.
(top and bottom) The decline of the "Green Sahara" started about 6000 years ago, concurrently with the beginning of human civilization in the region. Did humans cause this desert?

Janet Herman
Professor of Environmental Sciences and Director of Program of Interdisciplinary Research in Contaminant Hydrogeology (PIRCH), University of Virginia

Janet Herman began by suggesting that her work focuses on the disappearance of rock, not water, and went on to describe her research in geochemistry—the chemical reactions of rock. As President of the Karst Waters Institute, she began by identifying the regions of North America where the underlying bedrock is water soluable, including Florida and Mexico's Yucatan Peninsula, and spoke of her work on Florida's Gulf Coast (New Port Richey) and in Quintana Roo, Mexico.

She briefly described the process whereby limestone dissolves, when slightly acidic groundwater infiltrates soil, collecting to form the water table. As rainwater flows through limestone (calcium carbonate) it dissolves the limestone, carrying soluble chemicals away in the groundwater. As a result, the limestone becomes increasingly porous, leading to the formation of caves and eventually to the collapse of caves, known as sinkholes when they occur inland.

She explained that the water table slopes gently toward coastlines, where the freshwater table hits the barrier of denser saltwater, creating brackish water. She said that while the chemical properties of fresh and salt water mix linearly, the thermodynamic reaction is non-linear, leading to more rapid limestone dissolution near the coast. In a sense, the porosity of freshwater-saturated limestone draws saltwater inland, exacerbating the rate of collapse. As the freshwater table is depleted, saltwater intrudes inland at increasing rates, furthering the formation of shorelines and

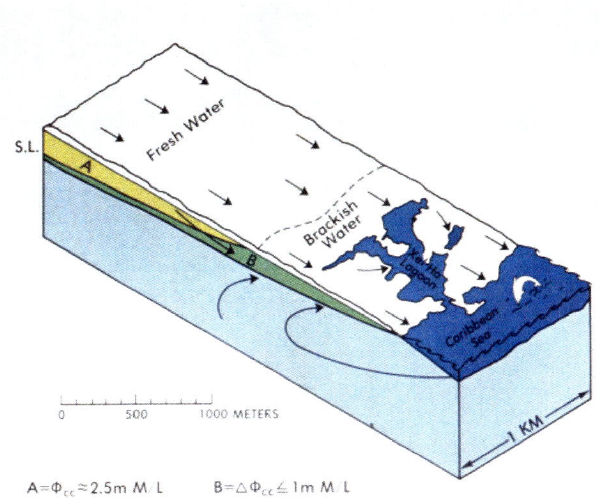

Geology, Diagram of freshwater, brackish water, and Caribbean.

saltwater intrusion still more rapidly. This leads to the formation of new coastal features—inlets or lagoons, as caves are formed and subsequently collapse into the sea.

In summary, she emphasized that her focus is the disappearance of rock, but that an outcome of this disappearance is the resulting decrease of freshwater through saltwater intrusion in coastal areas.

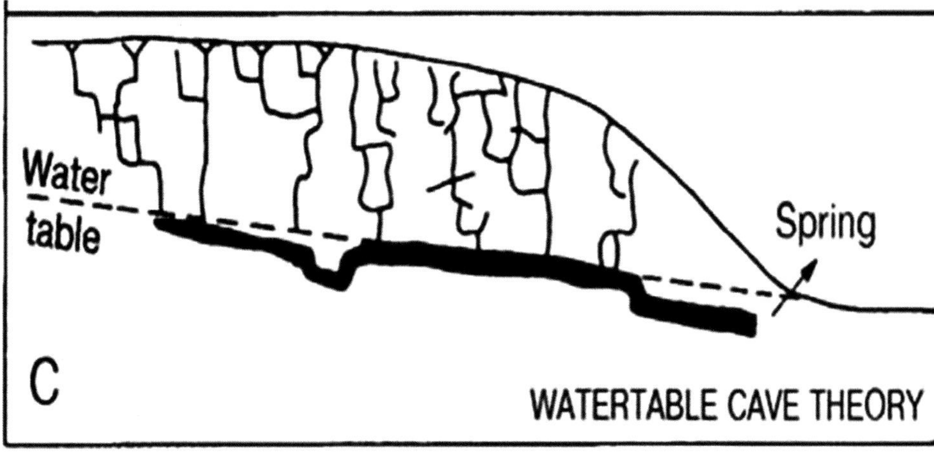

(left) GSA, Diagram of water table cave theory.
(right) USGS, Diagram of freshwater and saltwater.

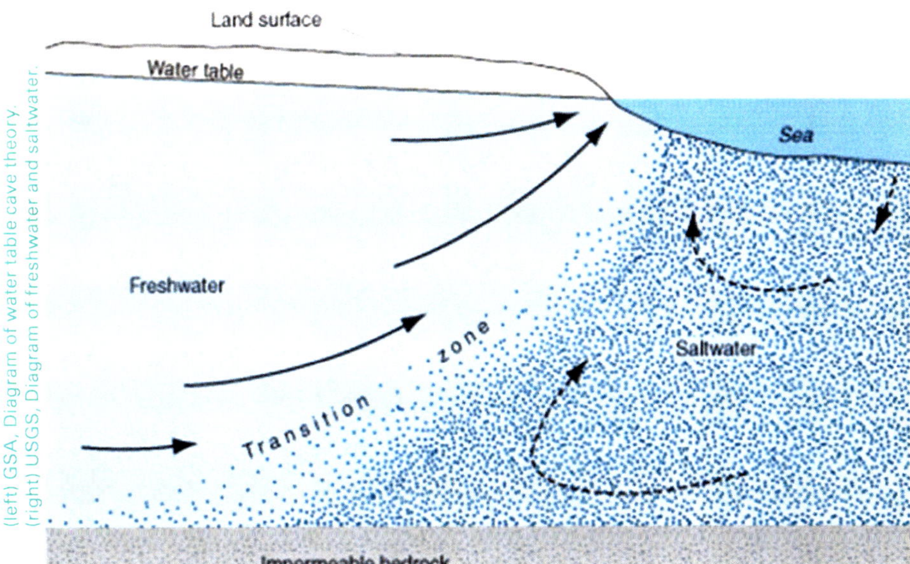

Brian Richter
Director of Global Freshwater Strategies of the Nature Conservancy and Lecturer, School of Architecture, University of Virginia

Richter began his presentation by proclaiming that "we all love water," saying we depend on it for human health and for habitats for other creatures. He reminded the audience that the disappearing sources of water negatively impact humans and all creatures dependent on water for their habitats. Extending the well known phrase, "if you build it they will come," he admonished, "if you destroy it they will disappear." His professional passion has been driven by his love of animals along with his love of water, particularly rivers.

He described two endangered river systems, the Colorado River in the western United States and the Murray River in Australia. He began with the well documented story of the Colorado River, beginning with a map showing the decline in flow between 1900 and 2010. He cited the extensive depletion of water due to farming, along with dams built to provide hydroelectric power, as two major causes of the diminution of the Colorado River, which no longer reaches the Pacific Ocean. He described 250 pound fish that formerly thrived in the Colorado River delta, and the adverse impact of the River's decline on other fish, as well as birds and native peoples of the region.

Moving to a discussion of the Murray River, Richter began by describing the "millennium drought" occurring between 1998 and 2010 in this region, which he characterized as the

Murray River, Australia.

breadbasket of Australia. He said river red gum trees died, some 300-400 years old, along with other vegetation. He argued that the river habitat was decimated by a combination of drought and overconsumption, and that it wiped out many aquatic species such as the Murray cod among others. He said farmers went broke, and some committed suicide, even taking their families with them to their graves. Richter's research focus is on the role human behavior might play in improving water quality and flow, with the ultimate goal of improving the multifaceted life of rivers.

Murray River, Australia. Reprint from *Chasing Water, A Guide for Moving from Scarcity to Sustainability.*

Water flows in the lower Colorado River have been heavily depleted by agricultural irrigation and urban water consumption, resulting in considerable damage to the river ecosystem and its species. This has in turn led to severe impacts on indigenous cultures dependent on fish and other resources in the delta. Colorado River, United States.

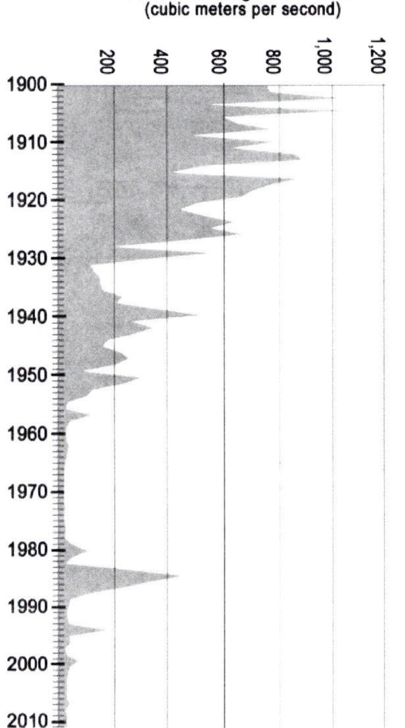

two

Comparison

"If I could tell you what it meant, there would be no point in dancing it."

Isadora Duncan

Here modern dance pioneer Isadora Duncan succinctly asserts the value of different forms of communication—dance expresses meaning in a way that words cannot. And so it is with images. The phrase "a picture is worth a thousand words" describes the immediacy of visual communication, suggesting it is not secondary or illustrative to text, but rather equally and powerfully meaningful in its own right.

Psychologist Howard Gardner, who developed the theory of multiple intelligences, explains that different tools are used by different people to think more clearly, either through language, images, movement, spatial reasoning, or sound. Across the four Dialogues, the varied and sometimes surprising modes of thinking employed by the presenters became evident. In reviewing each presentation and preparing this monograph, several visual themes emerged, common among the speakers. Each is presented comparatively on the pages that follow.

As I reflected on the similarities I uncovered, I realized they represent a continuum of knowing—from the abstract to the immediate. I was asked if these might be understood as a progression, starting from the experience of immersion and moving toward abstraction, or perhaps the reverse—moving from the analytic exercise of mapping toward full, embodied engagement. I leave this tantalizing question for others to consider.

Comparison: Mapping

Our presenters used maps to present information spatially, and to intensify meanings through color or other forms of symbolic emphasis. By redrawing known maps using different parameters, new relationships and opportunities become apparent. Here, Brian Richter showed a world map emphasizing the severity of aquifers' depletion, with the color red signaling the most severe problems. Margaret Tolbert redrew a map of Florida, defining boundaries through the contributing watersheds of freshwater springs, rather than traditional political boundaries. Phoebe Crisman demonstrated the act of changing spatial scales, zooming in from the entire multi-state Chesapeake watershed, to the Elizabeth River watershed, to her site at Money Point. Jim Smith used a web-based tool to show how a world map would morph to reflect the relative number of deaths from intestinal parasites, country by country.

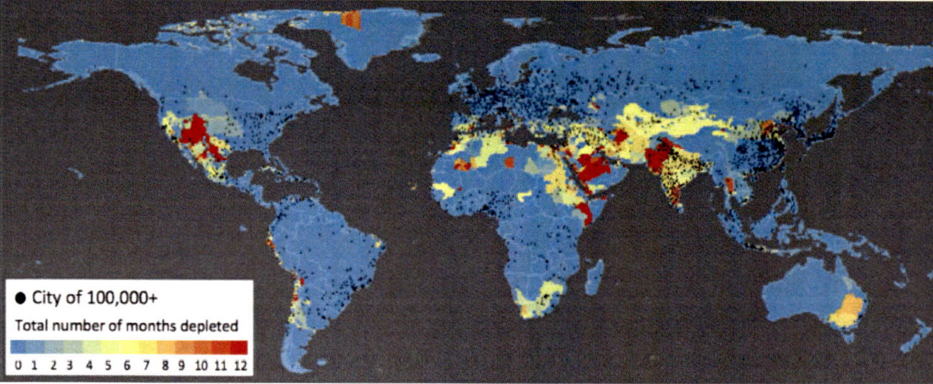

(left) Richter, Half of all cities with populations >100,000 are located in water basins in which more than half of available water supplies are being depleted during some portion of the year.
(right) Tolbert, Springsheds of Florida as political boundaries. Drawing, oil pastel, 2013, 12x18".

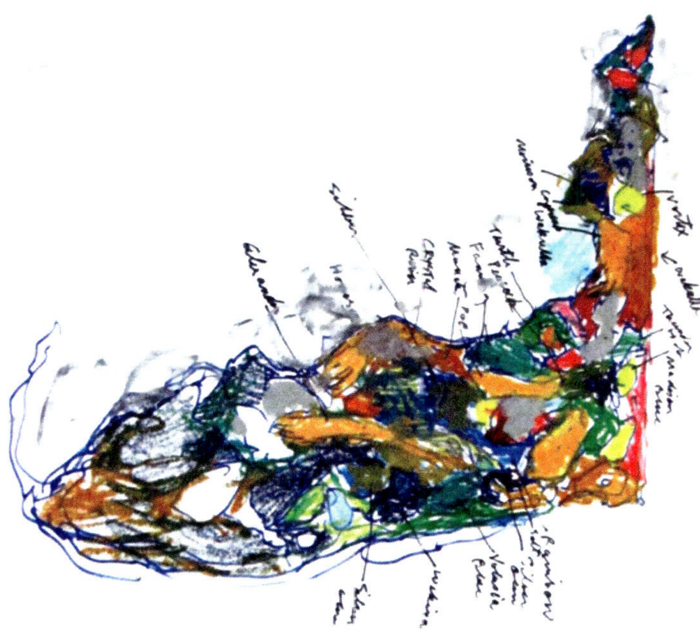

VICTORY BOULEVARD
SUMMER NE PREVAILING WINDS
JUN 21 SUNRISE 4:44AM

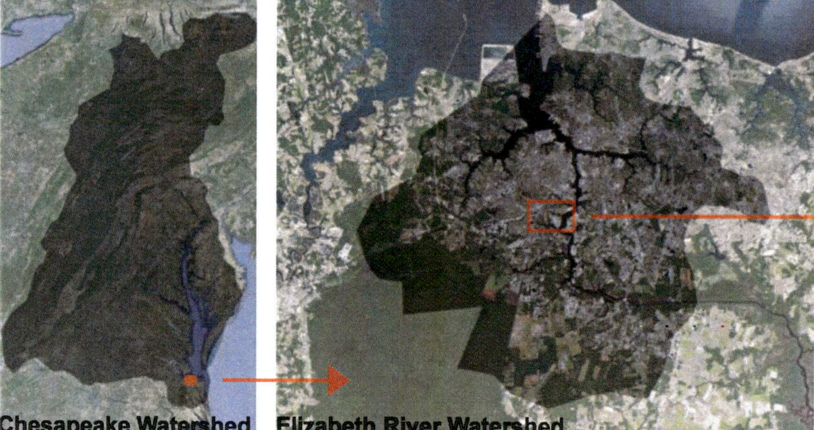
Chesapeake Watershed
Elizabeth River Watershed

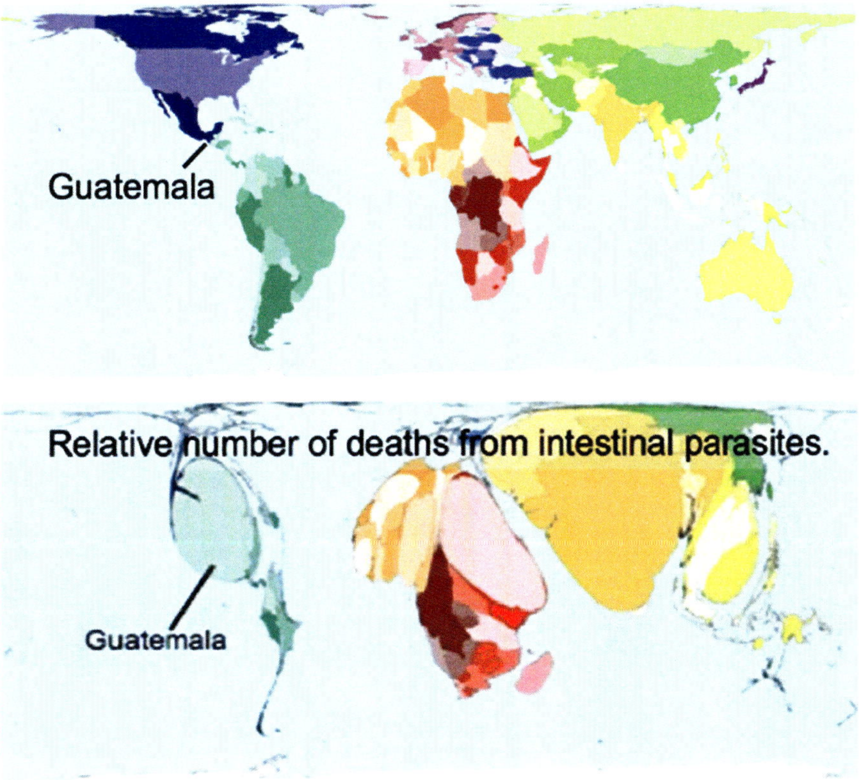

Guatemala

Relative number of deaths from intestinal parasites.

Guatemala

(left) Crisman, Paradise Creek Nature Park within the Elizabeth River Watershed within the Chesapeake Watershed.
(right) Smith, The world mapped according to numbers of deaths from intestinal parasites.

Comparison: Flows

Not surprisingly, given the subject of water, many of our speakers used images of flows. They ranged from evocative photographs and video clips to simplified abstractions of complex processes. Matthew Reidenbach showed, at a very small scale, an example of chemical dispersion by a coral reef, and he presented a video clip to explain how he maps flows using dye tests on the ocean's floor. Nana Last provided a diagram of the CERN Large Hadron Collider site, mapping the process of particle acceleration. Iñaki Alday used a famous diagram of the lower Mississippi River, demonstrating how floods could be controlled using a plumbing-like formal vocabulary. Brian Richter demonstrated the Colorado River's reduction in flow as it makes its way to the Pacific Ocean, explaining human overconsumption is largely responsible. Leonardo da Vinci's drawings demonstrate flows in several ways. He diagrammed the relationship between pressure and flow, mapped a river's flow across a landscape, and studied the behavior of water as it flows downstream.

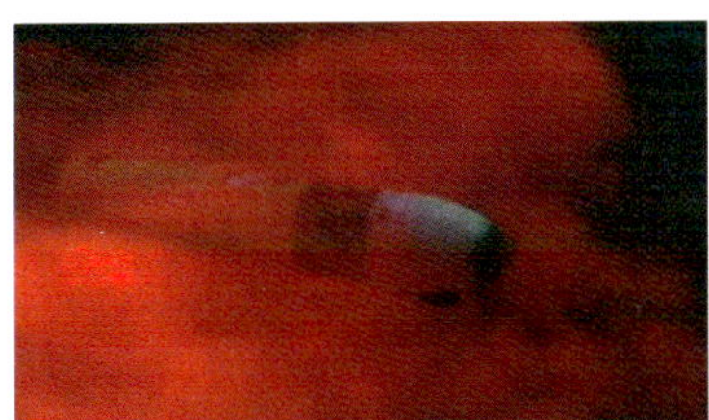

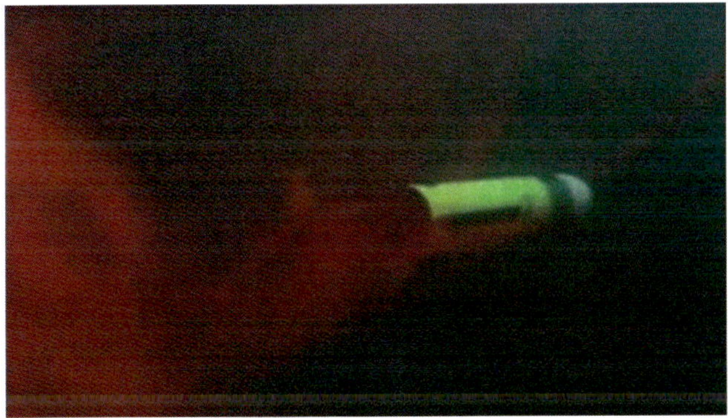

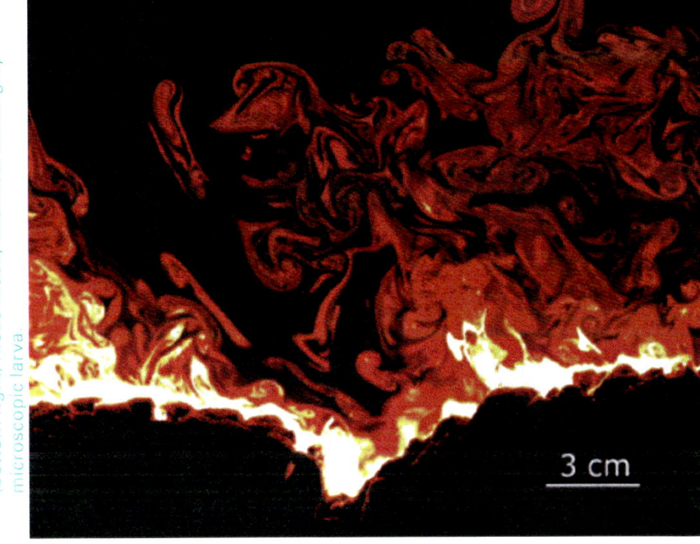

(top three) Reidenbach, Dye tests 1, 2, 3.
(bottom right) Riedenbach, Chemical sensing by microscopic larva.

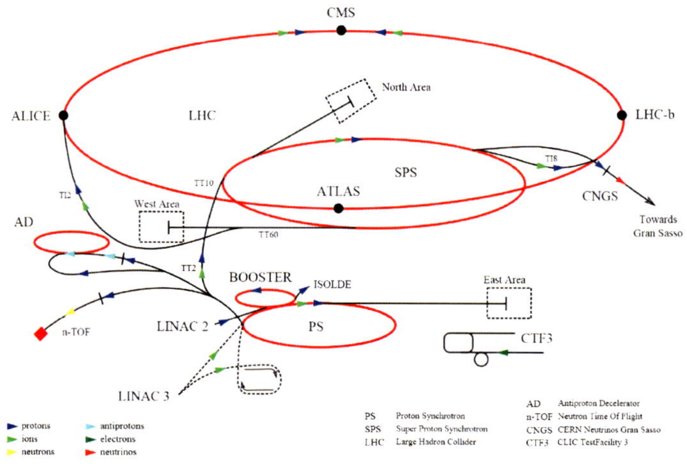

Colorado River Basin : Withdrawals and Consumption

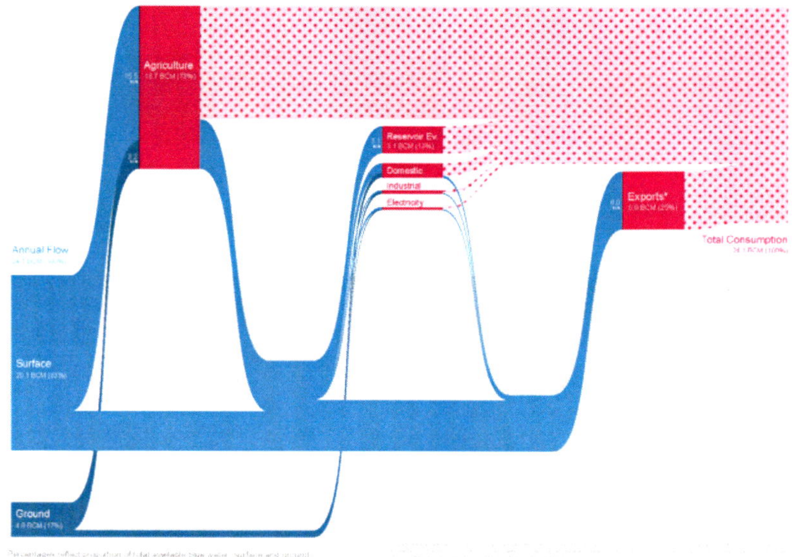

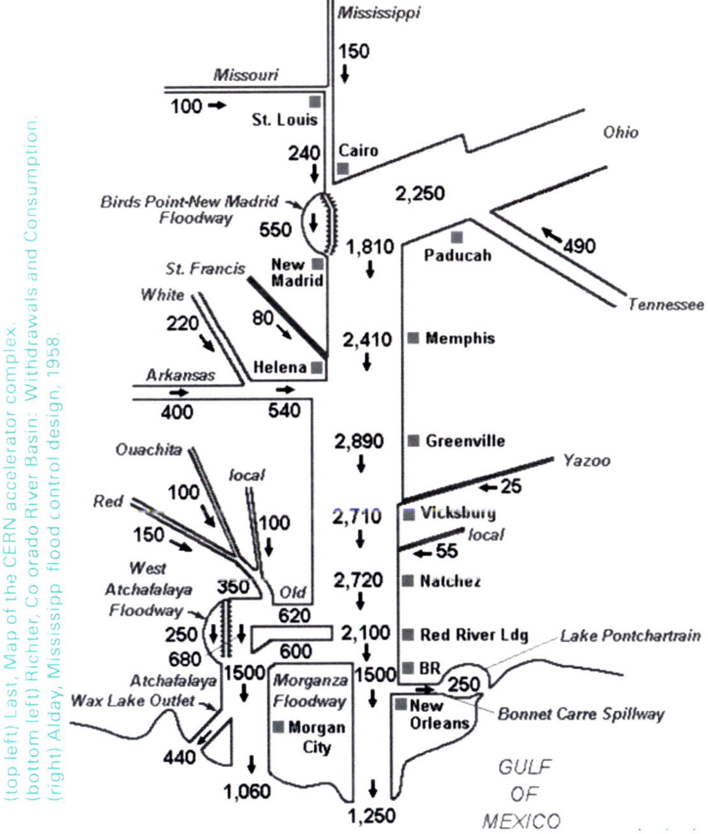

(top left) Last, Map of the CERN accelerator complex.
(bottom left) Richter, Colorado River Basin: Withdrawals and Consumption.
(right) Alday, Mississippi flood control design, 1958.

(left) Leonardo da Vinci in Geddes, Codex Atlanticus, c. 1509. Axonometric and section view of the Saint Christopher Shipway, Biblioteca Ambrosiana, Milan.
(middle) Leonardo da Vinci in Geddes, Water studies, c. 1507-09, Royal Library, Windsor Castle.
(right) Leonardo da Vinci in Geddes, Map of the river Arno.

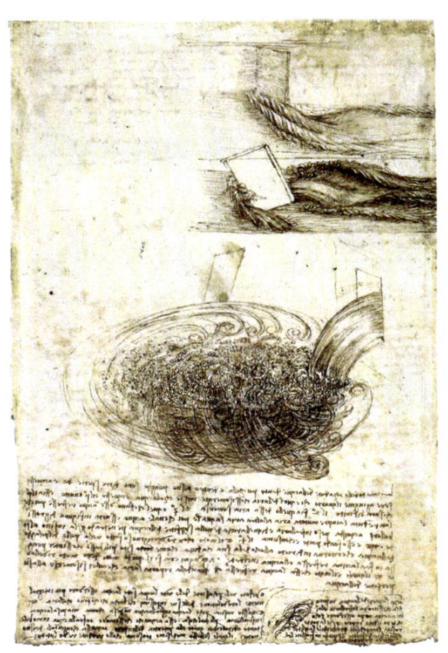

Comparison: Empathy

To a surprising degree, presenters' interest in water either grew from or evolved into a personal relationship with creatures they encountered. Margaret Ross Tolbert photographs and draws fish, turtles, and other creatures living in Florida's springs. Brandon Ballengée's life-long love of amphibians has moved him to devote his life's work to improving their watery habitats. Brian Richter's interest in rivers is motivated largely by his interest in protecting creatures from death and even species from extinction, as in his heartbreaking example of drought-stricken sheep in Murray, Australia.

(left) Richter, Murray River, Australia.
(middle) Ballengée, Amphibian deformities have been reported in six continents and appears to be increasing (at least among some populations).
(right) Tolbert, Lady fish, Silver Glen Springs.

Comparison: Immersion

Margaret Ross Tolbert's poem "Entering the Springs" led me to look for other forms of immersion. She writes in part,

> "I pause, suspended in the flow, then,
> sink
> into
> the depths,"

Here Tolbert beautifully describes the gradual, graceful act of immersing herself, becoming one with her subject of study. The word immersion comes from the Latin immergere—to dip into—making evident its aquatic origin. The other images in this sequence demonstrate different forms of immersion. Clearly Tolbert, swimming, is immersed literally in water. Ballengée, on the other hand, is engrossed in the experience of gathering samples with an equally eager group of schoolchildren. Burtner is immersed within a world of sound, closing his eyes so as to focus his attention on an acoustical flow.

(top) Burtner, Matthew Burtner in kayak. (bottom) Ballengée, Piedmont, Italy Eco-Action from 2010 Malamp IT studies. Image by Orietta Brombin, 2010.

(left) Margaret Tolbert swimming in spring. Image by Carlton Ward Jr/CarltonWard.com.
(right) Tolbert, "Entering the Springs" from *AQUIFERious* by Margaret Ross Tolbert.

Entering
the Springs
I enter the spring,
A WELL OF color, A POOL OF BRILLIANCE,
I pause, suspended in the flow, then,
sink
INTO
the DEPTHS,
into that flash of light at the bottom
where the water whips up BILLOWING sand clouds
as it emerges from subterranean passageways of the aquifer.

three

Reflection: The Practical Imagination

Francis Bacon, the 17th century philosopher, divided knowledge into three parts: Memory, Reason, and Imagination. Thomas Jefferson, following Mr. Bacon's work, divided his own library into three sections which he titled History, Philosophy, and Fine Arts. Mr. Jefferson's library formed the foundation for the Library of Congress.

Due to the persuasive power of Mr. Bacon's work, and that of his contemporary René Descartes, much of the intellectual effort of the last three hundred years has been devoted to the pursuit of reason. Known as the Age of Enlightenment, this period has led to the development of the scientific method, and to the 19th century development of the concept of science and scientists. That effort has focused on determining the cause of that which exists.

Left to atrophy in this quest for certainty has been the important role of imagination—that which might exist. Indeed, the fine arts, including architecture and oratory along with theater, painting, dance, and music, too often have been characterized as the self-expression of individual geniuses, only appreciated by connoisseurs. This proposal seeks to resuscitate the important third branch of Mr. Bacon's and Mr. Jefferson's organization of the world's knowledge, through the creation of a curriculum in practical imagination.

The need for a Curriculum in Practical Imagination

The limits of scientific thinking are evident all around us. Causality and replicability, two hallmarks of the scientific method, help us understand existing circumstances. Such circumstances can be predictive only if the conditions that led to them can be repeated. As systems theory teaches us, in the world this is the case only within bounded experiments or time or scale-limited real-life events. Several millennia ago, Heraclitus said, "You could not step twice into the same river, for other waters are ever flowing on to you." Science, by definition, has only a limited capacity to envision alternative futures, or to conceive of multi-faceted causality. While scientific method has led to great advances in our understanding of and ability to impact the world, it is time to rekindle the active and rigorous pursuit of the imagination.

Imagination can be generally defined as 1) the act or power of forming a mental image of something not present to the senses or never before wholly perceived in reality, 2) creative ability, the ability to confront and deal with a problem, the thinking or active mind, or 3) a creation of the mind or a fanciful or empty assumption (mirriam-webster.com). In current times, imagination is too often aligned with the third definition, and dismissed as a fanciful or empty assumption. In the same way, the fine arts, using Jefferson's term for this category of knowledge, are often disparaged as luxuries created to satisfy a small group of cultural elites. But the first definition, suggesting the ability to envision the future, or to make connections between unlikely things, holds underexplored promise. It is this use of the term imagination that suggests new avenues for interdisciplinary teaching and research at the University of Virginia.

The phrase "practical imagination" is a catachresis, or purposefully mixed metaphor. It conflates the improbability, beauty, and inspiration found in the arts with the dutiful resolve necessary in doing the world's work. While imagination is often viewed as impractical, the practical is too often unimaginative. The Curriculum in Practical Imagination seeks to celebrate this paradox and, in so doing, find a way to move past the regrettable dichotomy that often splits art from science, leaving both impoverished. At the same time it celebrates Mr. Jefferson's emphasis on useful knowledge.

First presented to the University's academic leadership August, 2010

*SYSTÈME FIGURÉ DES CONNOISSANCES HUMAINES.

ENTENDEMENT.

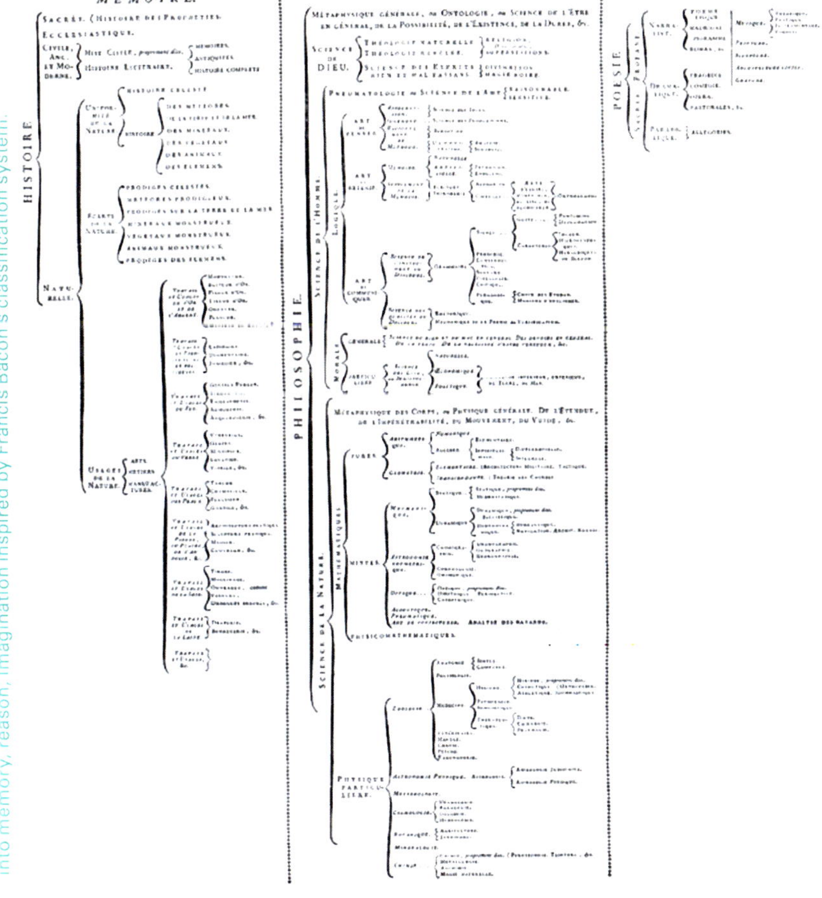

Tree taxonomy of knowledge from Diderot's 18th Century Encyclopédie. Knowledge is structured into memory, reason, imagination inspired by Francis Bacon's classification system.

Reflection: Dialogues Towards the Practical Imagination

"We know more than we can tell."

Michael Polanyi, in *The Tacit Dimension*, 1966, (p. 4)

Inspired by Leonardo da Vinci's comprehensive approach to the study of water, and by artist Margaret Ross Tolbert's combined aesthetic and activist commitment to the endangered freshwater springs of northern Florida, "After the Deluge, Reimagining Leonardo's Legacy," sought to juxtapose artistic and scientific practices in search of new holistic responses to one of today's major environmental challenges. The project was subtitled "a demonstration of the practical imagination applied to the ecology of water."

In inviting the Dialogues' presenters and introducing each session, I borrowed from the white paper "A Proposal to Create a Curriculum in Practical Imagination," (excerpted in this monograph) and provocatively asserted, "Science, by definition, has only limited capacity to envision alternative futures, or to conceive of multi-faceted causality. While the scientific method has led to great advances in our understanding of and ability to impact the world, it is time to rekindle the active and rigorous pursuit of the imagination."

I was quickly informed by one of our scientist-speakers, Pat Wiberg, that my dichotomy was overly simply. She argued that good scientists, like creators in any domain, are imaginative—something that quickly became clear as the Dialogues progressed.

P. Wiberg: I would say that one thing about science is that it is largely incremental, that somebody finds something, somebody else improves on it or expands it. But every now and then, somebody does just have an amazing insight that moves or shifts several things significantly and then everybody else catches up with them... I think it can be a great act of creativity to try to bring something that seems anomalous into a bigger framework of understanding

Each dialogue began with a plenary presentation followed by three or more shorter presentations, and each included a combination of artists, designers, theorists, and scientists. Following the presentations we had lengthy discussions, loosely structured by a series of four consistent questions. Titled "Dialogue Towards the Practical Imagination," I sought to find creative commonalities between the presenters, and to make overt what Polanyi describes as the "tacit dimension." What follows are some preliminary observations about common sources of creative inspiration, and my reflections about the difficulty of revealing the deep sources of imagination that motivate these exceptional creators.

How do you choose your subject matter?

Three themes recurred amongst many of the speakers. First, rich experiences from their childhoods often led to a life-long professional passion. Matthew Jull is Canadian by birth, and the Arctic has always held a special place in his imagination, as a remote frontier. Matthew Burtner, by contrast, grew up in the Arctic, and experienced its fierce beauty and harsh conditions as a child. He has sought to incorporate this primal inspiration into musical compositions. Phoebe Crisman grew up in Pennsylvania's Rust Belt, and found a surprising parallel in the Norfolk, Virginia region. Both Brian Richter and Brandon Ballengée expressed a childhood love of animals. Richter described his experience of the San Diego Zoo and especially his intense fascination with markers of species denoted "extinct" in the wild. Ballengée loved frogs as a child, and clearly still does. Both Richter and Margaret Tolbert have also loved the water since their childhoods—canoeing on it, swimming in it, and, in Tolbert's case, observing water's particular visual effects.

M. Jull: As a Canadian, there's a whole realm of the country that is very exciting but also very, growing up, a very unknown realm, and suddenly everyone's talking about and people are trying to fight over who's doing what, but I think really for me the Arctic is again, because it existed in our imagination for so long yet somehow it really is a frontier.

M. Burtner: For a long time, as a composer and a musician, I didn't really want to embrace my experiences growing up in remote places. You know, I grew up without electricity and running water in Alaska and the Arctic, and so I was kind of shy about that when I studied in Paris. My friends were all very cultured composers, exposed to very different, urban experiences, and so I kept those things quite separate, until I had a composition teacher named Julio Estrada, who treated composition and art as psychoanalysis. You look back into your childhood and you discover trends and unique aspects of your experiences and your personality, and you try to bring those out in the work as a way of being fruitful in art.

B. Richter: The first time I got on a moving body of water, in a canoe, that was all she wrote. That was it. That was the rest of my life. So I am madly in love with rivers.

Second, and not surprisingly given the academic context of the Dialogues, many presenters spoke with enthusiasm about the intellectual challenge they found in their work. Nana Last translated an interest in acts of speech into the performance of flows, framed by a deep knowledge of philosophy and physics. Hossein Haj-Hariri described the way he translates complex motion into equations, and Matthew Reidenbach described mapping currents' flows in the ocean. Rebecca Dillingham expressed a childhood fascination between science and society, found through the work of naturalist Stephen J. Gould. This translated into the study of the history of medicine then, following a trip to Africa, to studying medicine and public health. Janet Herman spoke enthusiastically of her interest in chemical reactions, and equally of her interest in being in the water.

J. Herman: I'm interested in chemical reactions. I just like to understand how it is that they proceed. And in geology, limestone is a very reactive rock with regard to water. Things happen fast enough to be able to measure it and observe it, so it's a nice topic to focus on if you want a result within your lifetime...And I also like water. I like swimming in creeks and rivers and diving springs and maybe having that transcendent experience of being in nature. So it was a good confluence of my academic preparation and my personal avocation of being outside.

Finally, many of the speakers aspire to make a difference. Not only do they love their subject matter, but they fear it is endangered and they have applied their professional training to attempt to stop or reverse man-made damage. Leena Cho expressed her profound surprise when she realized that the Arctic, which she had imagined as desolate, was populated by a rich variety of ethnic subcultures, potentially unaware of the political and economic changes likely to occur as the Arctic becomes navigable. Ballengée and Crisman both expressed the desire to have an impact on polluted sites, and to help future generations--today's children--understand the natural world through their own experience. Jim Smith redirected his research from what he described as mainstream environmental engineering to focus on waterborne pathogens in 2004, when he realized how profound this problem is, worldwide.

B. Ballengée: ... it was more just a love of organisms, a love of amphibians, a love of other animals, and just being very concerned, being alive at this particular moment in history, you choose to try to have an impact...

P. Crisman: The idea of making it something I care about: I care about the planet, I care about the kids that are growing up and will become stewards. I never thought that I would be focusing so much on the role of architecture and environment, restoration and education, but it's because it's relevant.

How do you think about your subject, and how do you externalize your thoughts? Through words? Images? Numbers? Sound? Motion? Space?

Here the presenters' answers were often surprising and sometimes oblique.

While I had anticipated that artists would describe thinking in pictures and engineers would think through numbers and equations, for example, it became clear that each discipline's expected form of communication was a necessary final step, but often not the realm in which their imaginations operated. Haj-Hariri and Smith described the kinetic spatiality of fluids with a choreographer's specificity, and both stated that they translated a kinetic understanding into equations in a subsequent stage of their processes. Herman explained that she thinks at a very small—indeed molecular—

scale, and described this world visually, as if she lived at that scale. Both Leslie Geddes and Francesca Fiorani toggle between verbal and visual thinking—seeing evidence in art and expressing it verbally, or understanding the context of Leonardo's art through others' research, then confirming it or refuting it through their own primary, visual examination of Leonardo's drawings and paintings.

H.Haj-Hariri: I actually go into the flow. I'm actually the particle in that flow that he has drawn, and I'm experiencing the stretch, I'm experiencing the turning, I am intertwining with my neighboring particles, and we're all moving. And I actually have my hands held out this way [spread out to sides] and depending on how the flow goes, maybe my hands come close together, maybe I'm rotating. So, that's the experience that you get when you look at nature. And to me that's imagination to some level. So that becomes science. But then engineering to me becomes layered imagination.

J. Herman: ... I've identified that I think at the very small scale. I really do think of a chemical reaction of a CO2 gas molecule becoming hydrated and then dissociating and being carbonic acid and a proton sitting down on a calcite mineral surface and dissolving.

Iñaki Alday and Pat Wiberg spoke about the role of visual representation. While Alday uses visual materials made by other architects as source materials, Wiberg thinks of visual evidence as a compelling way to make a point. She remarked on how visually arresting she found Burtner's film presentation.

Several presenters did provide immediate, more expected responses. Tolbert explained that she always thinks visually, though she also writes poetry and does performance pieces incorporating dance and motion as well. Burtner seems especially attuned to sound. Crisman described using words, drawings, more technical design frameworks, and full scale construction to externalize ideas, often working with students.

Both Crisman and Dillingham spoke of teaching as a particular means of externalizing thoughts. These speculations, made offhandedly as part of broader answers, merit further attention, and I will provide some initial observations in the conclusion of this section.

R. Dillingham: ...perhaps the way I externalize is through my mentorship and my working with students. And certainly, I don't teach a lot of, I don't really teach lecture classes because I'm a practicing physician, so if I teach it's in the clinical sphere, but do a lot of mentoring with global, experiential learning and projects, and in that way I try to transmit.

Finally, a number of presenters spoke of the academic criteria to "publish or perish" and mentioned that writing peer-reviewed articles, sometimes for a surprisingly diverse range of disciplinary journals, was a means of externalizing their thoughts. It would be fair to say that none of the presenters seemed to consider journal papers to be a primary form of creative expression.

Crisman explained that the Learning Barge is, itself, an idea made visible for others to see.

Ballengée described using gallery exhibitions and field trips with citizen scientists in the same way.

P. Crisman: How do you make these issues visible? That's where the environmental education and the Learning Barge idea came about... (H)ow do we actually let people know what we've done, because a lot of these water issues are kind of invisible.

It also became clear that many of the presenters had not, themselves, considered the preferred medium through which their imaginations moved.

What is your research method or creative process? Does it vary greatly from project to project?

Many, but not all, said they began with field observation, then moved to a laboratory or studio setting. Herman collects physical samples, then moves to the laboratory to analyze them. Paolo D'Odorico remarked that he was trained as an engineer, but now does field work because of his academic appointment in the Department of Environmental Sciences. He moves from theory to observation then back to the laboratory, using the scientific method "to quantify things." For Tolbert and Burtner, "fieldwork" is essential, though both do considerable processing of their source material in their studio environments. Richter said that while he looks at spreadsheets and flow charts, he has found that interpersonal, human interaction is also essential.

J. Herman: I think my methods are pretty consistent. That I go to the field, I collect samples of water, I analyze them chemically. I collect samples of the rock, I analyze them mineralogically. I use the tools of equilibrium thermodynamics to conceptualize reactions in the system. But then, apart from that field-based approach, one can also speculate.

P. D'Odorico: I was trained as a civil engineer, so when I first arrived at U.Va. my experience had been more theoretical, more based on theories and models, and then in working with the environmental sciences, it's much more useful to have a direct approach with direct observations. So lately, now, I spend one or two months a year in the field so I can put all of the experiences together.

Two presenters, Smith and Crisman, began differently. Smith said he works with students, developing a hypothesis then testing it in the laboratory environment. Only then does he take his work to the field, and he noted that ideas generated in the lab do not necessarily work in the field. Crisman said the project's scale determines her method. Looking at a watershed requires the use of abstract mapping techniques such as GIS, while field visits are more appropriate in considering site specific design projects. She also noted the importance of collaborating with others, which tends to add complexity to what would otherwise be a more predictable method.

J. Smith: My students and I are experimentalists, we do lab experiments, and I think the coolest thing is if you have a hypothesis, you think you know what's going to happen and you want to test it, and when the hypothesis is wrong, that is when you start thinking, "what am I missing here? What's going on that I didn't know about?" And...it may not be what you wanted when you started out, it's what leads to some of the most interesting results...Becca (Dillingham) and I see that, as we do get on these great ideas in the lab and then we go to the field with communities and they may or may not work. And it's just a completely different set of issues.

A third variation, where a question is developed and fieldwork, or site visits, are more episodic, was present among the architects and landscape architects. For Alday/Jover and Jull and Cho, visits to the site to record information are part of a more expansive form of research, or gathering of source materials. For Alday, case studies of other flooded sites was likely useful, while Jull and Cho drew information from economic and political realms, including the then-recently released WikiLeaks.

Although the type of data collected in the field varied, most participants collected information in its context, then returned to a more comfortable environment to process it and to transform it.

Many presenters described their involvement with other people, including community groups, citizen activists, policy-makers, and residents, sometimes in dire need of assistance, stating that they learned from the individuals and communitie with whom they worked. Dillingham spoke of her work in clinical field settings, which helped her understand her clients' needs in a way similar to the method used by Crisman and Ballengée.

In describing their research method, the presenters consistently made note of the importance of surprise. They relished having their hypotheses disproved, and often operated at the edge of discomfort, seeming to thrive on the unexpected directions in which their subject matter led them. Ballengée said he tries to "let the numbers speak for themselves and see what kind of story they tell," and that he tries to apply the same openness in his art as in his science.

M. Burtner: What we can look at is, do you feel, are you scared of this? Is this something you've just created that you're not sure about? And that's actually a very good place to be as an artist, being terrified of something, because it means you've actually doing what you set out to do. If you're comfortable and you know what you're doing, it's crap.

What connections do you find between your work and that of your colleagues involved in today's dialogue?

The obvious connection, and the one orchestrated by way of the presenters' invitations to participate, was in their subject matter. For example, the concept of fluidity, whether demonstrated in Leonardo's drawings (Geddes) or leading to a fascination with vaporized water (Fiorani) or used to prompt new architectural questions (Last) obviously and purposefully linked presentations within each Dialogue. Presenters dealing with contamination had much in common, as did those working on disappearing water. Floodwaters, which included sea level rise, ice melt, and river flooding, were more disparate in cause and therefore in response.

Second, the presenters noted their shared reliance on field work and collecting data, as described above. Cho compared Burtner's sound data, Wiberg's water data, and their use of photography in the Arctic. They discussed the complication of collecting data that did not confirm the hypothesis or the project's intended direction. For example, Alday remarked that the flood that overtook their project site had to be accepted, perhaps as a form of "data," and incorporated as part of the project.

They also recognized their shared challenges of working in the field, dragging equipment to remote locations and working in and under difficult circumstances. Burtner described the difficulty of traveling thousands of miles to do sound recordings, only to realize he had forgotten a simple but critical cable to connect pieces of equipment to each other. Wiberg described the logistics of fieldwork as a nightmare, saying it often has to do with "trying to take technology into the outdoors where it's not always happy." Herman reflected on the difficulty Tolbert must have painting in a kayak with a floating sidecar to hold her canvases. While acknowledging these challenges, it was clear that each presenter accepted them as necessary to accomplish their goals.

J. Herman: ...I can't have a water sample unless I go out and get it. But that image of you [Margaret] in the kayak with the floating sidecar of painting, that seemed like the hard way to go about it. Seemed like you could have gone out and developed some sort of idea of the spring and it would have been a lot easier to paint it at home.

M. Tolbert: You can, but it doesn't look the same.

Third, they noted the role experiential learning played in their work, and the importance they placed on engaging others experientially. Ballengée and Crisman, in particular, spoke about the importance of drawing children into natural settings to experience the world unmediated by today's technologies.

B. Ballengée: We're getting a lot of information through secondary experience rather than primary experience. I'm really interested in exploring that, through just bringing people out and doing very physical activity and just visual investigation. Handling things, holding a tadpole in your hands for the first time and feeling and looking at it.

Not surprisingly, the presenters in each Dialogue were clearly curious and became deeply engaged in each others' work. During the discussions they asked each other lively, thoughtful questions, and several cross-disciplinary, cross-country collaborations have evolved out of the Spring 2013 "After the Deluge" project.

B. Richter: You know, there is a flip side to what Margaret said. She said how she benefits from having the science there, as part of her team in advocacy or in trying to change policies. Well most scientists are quite frustrated. If scientists care about the world, they are quite frustrated by their inability to influence policy decisions, as you very well know. And I think having someone who can speak to the broader humanities, to appeal to the aesthetic, to appeal to the artistic tendencies can make us a lot more effective. So I think we really should be looking for ways to complement each other more effectively.

Imagining an integrated whole

"We can see now how an unbridled lucidity can destroy our understanding of complex matters. Scrutinize closely the particulars of a comprehensive entity and their meaning is effaced, our conception of the entity is destroyed."

Polanyi, *The Tacit Dimension*, (p. 18)

The demonstration "After the Deluge: Reimagining Leonardo's Legacy" took as its inspiration from Western civilization's archetypal integrator, Leonardo da Vinci, and further focused on his studies and speculations about water. As Leslie Geddes and Francesca Fiorani beautifully described, Leonardo explored water from many perspectives: He boiled millet seed to see turbulence in action. He drew rock formations to understand water's slow removal of material through erosion. He designed watercourses to minimize floods, and experimental devices to understand water's force. He externalized his imagination in various ways. According to Geddes, "Perceiving phenomena that are fleetingly transient or imperceptibly gradual led Leonardo to divergent modes of representation, one analytical, the other poetic." As several of our "Deluge" speakers remarked, Leonardo was an artist, an engineer, a scientist, and a poet. Some speakers compared their modes of production to portions of Leonardo's efforts, though none suggested their work matched his unparalleled genius.

What became apparent through the Dialogues is the degree to which most of our speakers depend on multiple ways of knowing, and on multiple forms of knowledge. It is also clear that the professional formats in which speakers' present their work—from art exhibits to scientific papers—are not necessarily aligned with their primary way of imagining. In addition, for many presenters, the act of knowing through their own embodied experience, was both a source of initial inspiration and remains an ongoing means of learning. While scientists typically profess dispassionate objectivity, and artists clearly define objective methods to guide their creative work, in fact both scientists and artists inflect their professional output toward what they perceive to be preferred futures. Our presenters—both the artists and the scientists—in effect described the creation of "mental images of something not present to the senses or never before wholly perceived in reality." Through the Dialogues I learned that Bacon's third branch of knowledge, Imagination, is intact and thriving, no matter the domain.

Michael Polanyi, whose brilliant 1966 book titled *The Tacit Dimension* prefigured Thomas Kuhn's *The Structure of Scientific Revolutions*, describes the process of learning, the meaning of knowledge, and the role imagination plays in moving from the known to the possible. The full text provides an argument that is subtle and persuasive. Here I offer a few tantalizing hints of his argument to reintegrating our world, following Leonardo's example. Polanyi describes the importance of tacit knowing, which allows us to incorporate knowledge through our bodies. He calls this "indwelling" saying, "To interiorize is to identify ourselves with the teachings in question..." As an example he suggests, "This is why mathematical theory can be learned only by practicing its application: its true knowledge lies in our ability to use it." (p. 17) He goes on to describe how fields of knowledge are built, and the role of teaching and professional "gatekeepers" in determining what knowledge is to be adopted and what is to be overlooked or rejected. He cautions against what he describes as moral skepticism and moral perfectionism, and identifies these dampening qualities in post-Enlightenment scientific thinking. He reminds us of the ongoing creation of the world, saying "nothing that *ought* to be, can be determined by knowing what is." (p. 44)

Participants in "After the Deluge," through their lively, accessible presentations, and by sharing their personal stories and ways of working, demonstrated that for them, knowledge emerges, indwells, and moves toward "something that has never before been wholly perceived in reality" or "something that *ought* to be." Their shared focus on water provided a common matrix for discussion. Because only the boundaries of their own skins separate the watery environments within each of them from the object of their professional and personal passions, the Demonstration presented a refreshingly fluid exchange.

"After the Deluge: Reimagining Leonardo's Legacy" demonstrated that reintegrating the world's knowledge is not only possible--the project is well underway.

four

Exhibition: AQUIFERious VIRGINIA

The exhibit AQUIFERious VIRGINIA featured Gainesville, Florida-based artist Margaret Ross Tolbert's paintings, drawings and digital installations. A source of inspiration for the "After the Deluge" project, Tolbert's work fuses an artist's sensibilities, an environmentalist's concern, a citizen's activism, and an athlete's kinetic awareness, in a joyful alchemy devoted to protecting Florida's freshwater springs. The exhibit included oil paintings, lenticular photography, and portions of her award-winning book, *AQUIFERious*.

Tolbert was keynote speaker in the public dialogue "After the Deluge: the Disappearing," which took place on Friday, March 29th, at the U.Va. School of Architecture. This was the fourth and final event in "After the Deluge: Reimagining Leonardo's Legacy."

Margaret Ross Tolbert received her B.F.A. and M.F.A. from The University of Florida. Having participated in residencies all over the world, and with numerous solo exhibitions completed, Margaret Ross Tolbert has turned her attention to issues pertaining to water, particularly to springs. In 2010, Ms. Tolbert released a book of her artwork and writings about the freshwater aquifers of Florida titled, *AQUIFERious*, which garnered a gold medal in

(all images) AQUIFERious VIRGINIA exhibit, Dean's Gallery, 2013.

the State of Florida's annual non-fiction competition, along with a silver medal in fine arts. This book exemplifies Tolbert's interdisciplinary approach to her artwork. Her work is held in private, institutional, and public collections in Europe and across the United States. More information about Margaret Ross Tolbert and her work and research may be found on the website: www.margaretrosstolbert.com.

About the Dean's Gallery

The Dean's Gallery was launched in the fall of 2009 by Dean Kim Tanzer with the goal of celebrating the School's legacy of drawing and making. At Tanzer's invitation, Sanda Iliescu, Associate Professor of Architecture and Art, has served as Curator of the Dean's Gallery since its inception. The gallery has hosted more than a dozen exhibitions over the past five years. Shows have included work by architects Manuel Bailo Esteve, WG Clark, Edward Ford, and Mark West, landscape architect Michael Vergason, visual artists Pam Black, Lauren Catlett, Dean Dass, Sanda Iliescu, and Hana Kim, fabric designer Katie Wood, and composer Natalie Draper, along with Margaret Ross Tolbert.

As described by Iliescu, "In its selection of artwork and architectural drawings, the Dean's Gallery seeks to cultivate a sense of diversity and intellectual openness. While it displays work done in a range of mediums and methods, the gallery aims to highlight works in particular that are made by hand. It is tempting to abandon the practice of making models, sketches, and drawings by hand in today's world of advanced digital technology. While the gallery values these new approaches, it seeks to celebrate the importance of the human hand – and of multisensory experience generally – as essential elements in the design process.

The Dean's Gallery consists of three adjacent display areas: the public lobby outside the dean's office, the office of the dean's assistant, and the office of the dean. In addition to exhibiting artwork and architectural drawings, sketches and collages of distinction, the gallery aims to make the dean's office an open and welcoming public space."

AQUIFERious VIRGINIA was guest curated by Kim Tanzer, Silvi Steffi, and Cynthia Smith.

acknowledgements

"After the Deluge: Reimagining Leonardo's Legacy" was a complicated and rich project, requiring the support, good will, and inspiration of many people. George Sampson, Lecturer in the School of Architecture, worked tirelessly to fundraise, make connections across Grounds and to help coordinate the events of Spring 2013. Sampson also mentored Caroline Gonya, a U.Va. Arts Administration major, who provided logistical assistance and transcribed the many hours of video to make them useful for this document. Jody Kielbasa, Vice Provost for the Arts, was a game co-sponsor earlier in his term. Open Grounds provided a meeting space for our larger planning meetings, and Lindsey Hepler deserves a special thanks for her help in arranging this venue for our use. Matthew Pinyan and Charles Sparkman both provided much needed, just-in-time backup on many occasions. Cally Bryant, as always, made vague ideas beautiful, no matter how little time she had available. Cynthia Smith, as always, wore many hats. She facilitated events, managed publicity, supervised the installation and coordination of Margaret Ross Tolbert's exhibition "AQUIFERious VIRGINIA," and served as a frequent sounding board and constant intellectual collaborator. Thomas Woltz encouraged the project early on and has translated his initial enthusiasm into wonderful design prospects. Funding for the project was provided by the Fiddlehead Fund, a grant from the University of Virginia Arts Council, and a grant from the Vice Provost for the Arts, I am extremely grateful for their generous support. All of our presenters—throughout the University of Virginia and across the country—were tremendously good sports as we sought to bridge disciplinary silos and to find shared sources of inspiration. Finally, for her talent, intelligence, passion, and friendship, I would like to thank Margaret Ross Tolbert, whose multi-dimensional career has served as a source of inspiration to me for many years.

Kim Tanzer, FAIA
Dean and Edward E. Elson Professor
June 2014
Charlottesville, Virginia

author

Kim Tanzer FAIA has served as the Dean and Edward E. Elson Professor of Architecture at the School of Architecture at The University of Virginia for a five-year term beginning in 2009. She was elected to the American Institute of Architecture College of Fellows in 2011, and named a Distinguished Professor by the Association of Collegiate Schools of Architecture in 2014. She has served as president of the Association of Collegiate Schools of Architecture and founding president of the National Academy of Environmental Design.

At U.Va., Dean Tanzer has worked to enhance the School's design research culture, in part by creating a new interdisciplinary Ph.D. in the Constructed Environment. She led the School's 2012-13 interdisciplinary focus on the theme of water, titled "DRINK," of which "After the Deluge: Reimagining Leonardo's Legacy" was part.

Much of Dean Tanzer's teaching and research focuses on the relationship between the human body and large shared spaces such as the city and the landscape, with an emphasis on creating sustainable environments. She is co-editor of *The Green Braid: Towards an Architecture of Ecology, Economy, and Equity*, and has authored many scholarly and popular articles.